ALAN TITCHMARSH

THE

GARDENER'S
L O G B O O K

ALAN TITCHMARSH

THE

GARDENER'S
LOGBOOK

Willow Books
Collins
Grafton Street, London
1985

Willow Books
William Collins & Co Ltd
London Glasgow Sydney Auckland

Titchmarsh, Alan, 1949 –
The gardener's logbook
1. Gardening
I. Title
635 SB450.97

ISBN 0 00 218183 5

First published 1985
Copyright © Alan Titchmarsh and Lennard Books 1985

Made by Lennard Books
Mackerye End, Harpenden
Herts AL5 5DR

Editor Michael Leitch
Designed by David Pocknell's Company Ltd
Illustrations by John Woodcock
Production Reynolds Clark Associates Ltd
Printed and bound in Spain by
TONSA, San Sebastian

Contents

Introduction

Since the age of fourteen, when I was given my first 'Gardener's Diary', I have been a dramatic failure at chronicling any events that have taken place on the earth outside my various homes. I could usually manage to stagger through to the middle of January, recording such gripping pieces of information as: 'Cloudy and miserable. Went for a walk with the dog,' but such copy is hardly in the Samuel Pepys mould.

However, one diary, also filled in until only 20th January, marks the time I started work on the local nursery. It contains such gems as: 'My turn on boilers so I did them.' An innocent enough phrase, but one that, for me, conjures up vivid images of a five-foot-nothing youth swinging on the end of an eight-foot steel poker as he prised the clinkers from a solid fuel boiler large enough to power the Royal Scot, were its energy not needed for heating the fourteen greenhouses to which it was coupled. I wish I'd written more.

I wish I'd written more, too, in the back of my first gardening encyclopaedia, where I penned in a round, schoolboy hand: 'May 30th, peonies coming into bloom in the garden of the last house on my paper round.' I can see that grey-soiled border now, and those orbicular buds of green and crimson ready to burst, and I can feel the weight of the bag, too.

But enough of nostalgia. It's time to do something about this failing, and to make sure that in future years I have not only memories to fall back on, but useful snippets of information that will save me time and money.

Hence *The Gardener's Logbook*. Don't sigh at the responsibility that falls upon your shoulders on receipt of this volume. It's nicely printed, smartly turned out, and a prime candidate for the coffee table or the bookshelf. But if that's where it stays you'll be missing out.

It longs to be filled in; to be privy to your best and your worst thoughts on gardening. If you tell it that the grouping of plants at the far end of your left-hand flower border is appalling, it will remind you of the fact later in the season and goad you into changing the scheme.

It will cheer you up in later years when you see how a planting has developed from those early years when it looked raw and unexciting. It

will help you to spot crop failures, too. By detailing the performance of plants – be they vegetables for the pot or roses for the vase – you'll be able to spot the winners and the losers and fill your garden with the plants that most generously repay your efforts.

This is not a book that's finished with at the end of its first year. There are pages to fill in over succeeding years as the garden matures, and things like bulb plans that remain relevant as long as your garden exists.

You'll need little skill to fill in the pages, but you'll need a bit of imagination when it comes to designing your plot, and a bit of care when you're writing or drawing. On some pages a soft pencil is the best bet; it gives you a chance to change your mind and rub out ideas that once seemed good but now seem odd. For logging the performance of your plants choose something more permanent. Ballpoint? Fine felt-tip? Rolling writer? Or that acme of calligraphic perfection, the fountain pen? It's up to you.

While you're doing your best to live up to the demands of this book, rest assured that I'll be doing the same, and when the going gets tough, take time to sift through the quotes from famous gardeners ancient and modern. One quote is missing, and that's the one from Dorothy Parker. It was she who penned the most cutting critique of all time; 'This is not a book to be tossed aside lightly; it should be thrown with great force.'

Stay your hand. And enjoy your garden.

THE
GARDENER'S
L O G B O O K

—— NAME ——

—— ADDRESS ——

—— TELEPHONE ——

The Garden Surveyed

The term 'surveying' has such a grand sound to it that it's bound to put off any gardener who doesn't know a theodolite from a toxophilite. No matter. Even the most ham-fisted horticulturist can usually rough out a sketch plan, and that's all that's needed here. Just something to show you what it was like before you started, and how you *hope* it will look when you've finished.

When you're planning your patch, do think very carefully about what you want it to do for you. Aspect is the first consideration; which way is north? Keep your eye on the sun and see just which parts of the garden are drenched in it for most of the day – that bright spot is the place for your patio or sitting-out area. If you want a greenhouse, look again for a part of the garden that's not in shade.

Start off with a list of requirements: a lawn (but only where there's room for one – in small gardens areas of gravel or paving are far more practical); somewhere for the children to play; a rock garden; a pool; the washing line; a vegetable plot. Find a way of fitting them all in to a pleasing design – easily said but not always easily done.

Don't plan a garden that can be taken in with one brief glance. Create a few hidden corners that will tempt the curious to explore. Allow for a focal point or two – a small tree or a bit of statuary – to catch your eye in the far distance.

Landscape architects will offer you all sorts of complicated rules, but only a handful are of vital importance if you want a garden that's practical yet pleasing:

- Make it simple. Large sweeps of border and lawn make the tiniest garden look much larger. Twiddly bits can be hard on the eye and hard on the back when it comes to upkeep.
- Aim for a bit of year-round form with evergreens. Trees and shrubs are the backbone of any garden, so use them well.
- Look closely at the gardens around yours. Avoid buying plants that are obviously unsuited to the area (rhododendrons on limey soil, for instance) and you'll save a lot of time and money.
- Foliage is far longer-lasting than flowers, and much of it is brightly coloured, too. Rely on it.
- Be kind to your soil. What goes in must come up, so attend to soil drainage and enrichment before you plant a thing.
- Take your time. Plant up the bit of garden nearest to the house first of all. Gaze fondly on this and you can ignore the temporary chaos beyond (for a few years anyway!).

But all this doesn't help you much when it comes to deciding on a shape or plan. Neither does a blank piece of graph paper. What you need is something much more practical – a few garden canes, a bucket of sand, and a bedroom window to plot from. Lay trails of sand on the earth to mark out border curves and sweeps, and stick in canes to mark the position of trees. You'll need a bit of imagination, but it's far easier to line things up from the house as they will be seen than to map them in bird's-eye-view fashion on a plan.

When you're happy with the view from the window, that's the time to commit the plan to paper. It saves you all the bother of running round trying to find your trails of sand after a torrential downpour.

Land clearance

Of course, all this sand trail laying assumes that the earth is already clean, but when a gardener takes on a new plot that's seldom the case. Alas, there's no instant remedy for bedsteads and bindweed, brickbats and buttercups. Only hard graft will rid you of them. It's no use rotavating the lot – every chopped bit of weed root will survive, so consult your garden centre or nursery about a suitable weedkiller, unless you're happy to dig the lot out by hand.

Take heart; you'll get there in the end. And rest assured that every gardener on this earth thinks that his weed problem is worse than anybody else's.

Soil testing

The acidity of your soil governs what you can grow in it. Rhododendrons and azaleas love acid soil; pinks and clematis and irises enjoy alkaline soil. It all depends on how much lime there is in your earth. A simple soil test kit will tell you what's known as the pH value of your soil. Note it down here:

The Front Garden Now

Sketch out your front garden as it is now, and take some photographs, too. That way you'll see the bones of the place – or the lack of them. In a few years' time, when you've slaved and carved and planted and pruned, you'll have forgotten how much worse it looked at the start. The plan will remind you; and friends are terribly impressed by 'before and after' comparisons.

Depending on the size of your plot, use each square to represent one square foot, one square yard or even more if you own an estate.

Symbols

Tree   Deciduous shrub

Evergreen shrub   Border plants

BULBS

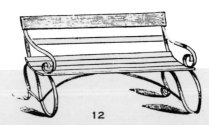

'The amount of old bedsteads, old plough-shares, old cabbage stalks, old broken-down earth
closets, old matted wire, and mountains of sardine tins, all muddled up in a tangle of
bindweed, nettles and ground elder, should have sufficed to daunt anybody.'
Vita Sackville-West on Sissinghurst
Journal of the Royal Horticultural Society (November 1953)

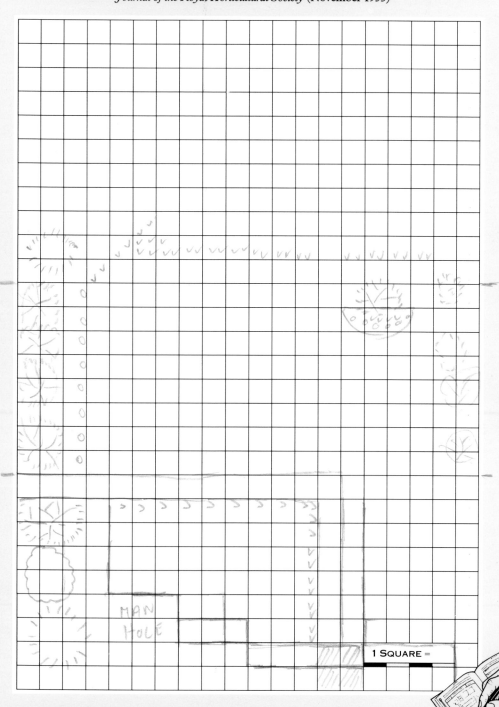

The New Front Garden

'He must have his own sketch map clear in his head before he starts to level or plant.'
Harold Nicolson (husband of Vita Sackville-West) in the Introduction to
Peter Coats's *Great Gardens of the Western World* (1963)

For some of us it's better if the sketch map is transferred from head to paper. Use a pencil. This is not *The Times* crossword. Here you're allowed to change your mind from time to time and make alterations.

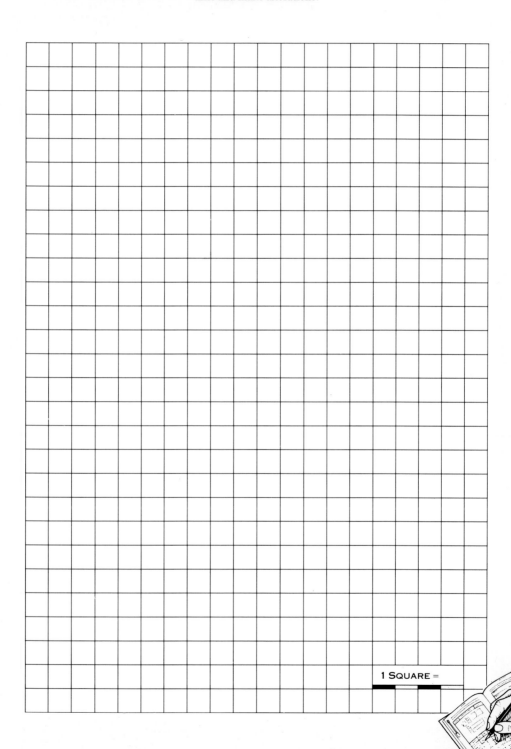

1 SQUARE =

The Back Garden Now

The back garden (and the vast majority of houses have one) is your own special, private, outdoor room. The front garden might set out to impress the neighbours; the back garden should set out to impress you. Sketch out its prominent features here, making special note of those to be kept.

Symbols

Tree   Deciduous shrub

Evergreen shrub   Border plants

'When the site is a bare field, or any place without individuality, the designer has a free hand, but will be wise in choosing something that will be definite, so as to give that precious quality of character.'
Gertrude Jekyll, *Gardens for Small Country Houses* (1912)

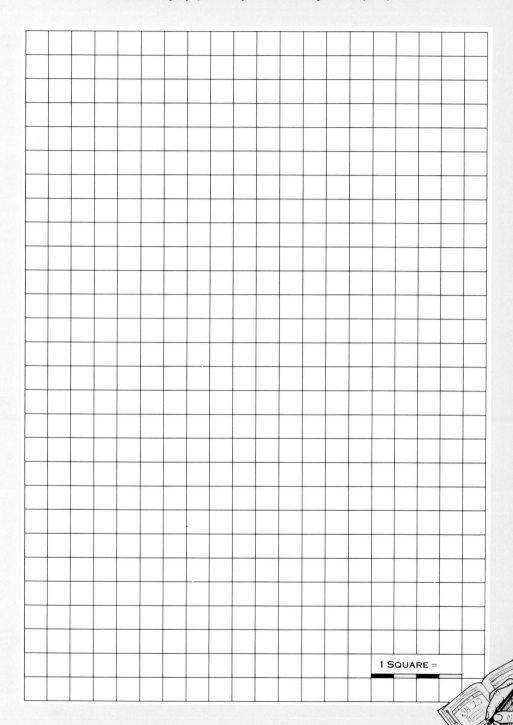

1 SQUARE =

The New Back Garden

Take up the pencil again and rough-out your ideas. Make the paths wide (you'll broaden as you age) and allow for some views along vistas (even if they're only ten feet from start to finish). Above all, plan and plant for privacy.

'You must be firm with yourself and leave room for some large groups, some broad effects.'
Christopher Lloyd, *The Well Tempered Garden* (1970)

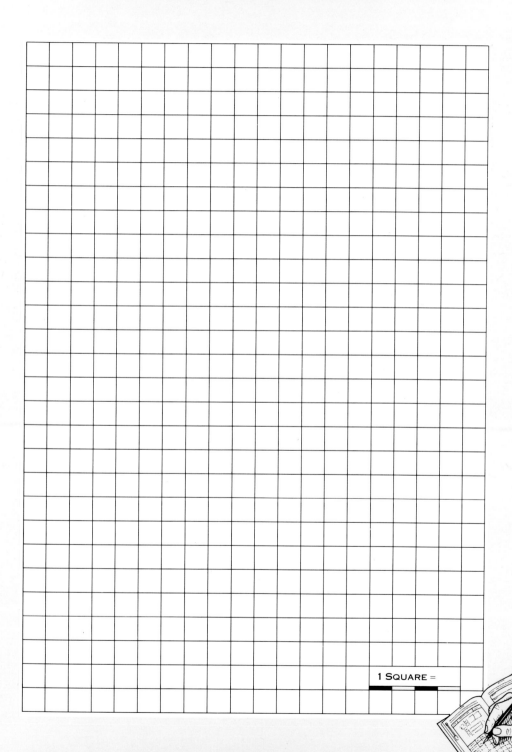

1 SQUARE =

The Toolshed

With an unlimited budget you can fill your toolshed with an armoury that would have made Henry VIII green with envy. There are peculiar poles with spikes on the end, or with rotating toothed wheels, that would have been far more effective than a simple halberd. Use them if you must. If you'd rather save money, then invest in a mere handful of the simplest tried and tested implements:

   – A spade
   – A fork (the small border kind is especially useful)
   – A rake
   – A Dutch hoe
   – A trowel
   – A pair of secateurs

These are the real essentials, and you can add to them when you feel the need.

Don't stint yourself and buy the cheapest, but on the other hand there's no need to buy stainless steel unless you're a millionaire who's taken a course in body building. Stainless steel tools are heavy on the arms as well as the pocket. I'd buy a stainless steel trowel for preference, but every other implement in my shed is made from plain old forged steel.

Choose an implement that's comfortable to handle – smooth of shaft and well balanced – and if it's at all possible, avoid buying a new one. Now there's a statement guaranteed to endear me to manufacturers! The thing is that well-used garden tools are so much easier to use than gleaming new ones. They've been broken in. That's why it's no bad idea to go round the aged members of your family inquiring (in the most tactful way possible) if they have finished with their spade and fork. They'll be a dream to work with.

Taking care

I know it takes real discipline to clean your spade when it's chucking down with rain; it's far easier to hang it up, mud and all, and come in to get warm. Resist the temptation. Scrape off the mud with a natty little implement made from a sawn-off dessert spoon, and then rub down the blade or the prongs or whatever with an oily rag. It only takes a minute and it makes the implements much easier to use next time round.

IMPLEMENT	SOURCE	PRICE	DATE BOUGHT
Potatoe Fork	Mum & Dad		20/3/93
Spade	'' ''		Sept- 93

Weather Records

> 'O Western Wind, when wilt thou blow
> That the small rain down can rain:
> Christ, that my love was in my arms,
> And I in my bed again.'
> Anon, *A Traveller's Poem* (16th century)

Never is one's memory more deceptive than in recalling the weather. Keeping a rough record of dryness, wetness, warmth and coldness of the months can be a great time and plant saver. If your carrots fail to emerge and your sweet peas flower badly check back on the weather and you might well discover the reason. A soggy seedbed? A drought at bud-forming time?

There's no need to buy elaborate bits of equipment, although enthusiasts will own a barometer, a maximum and minimum thermometer and a rain gauge at the very least. Sunshine recorders come rather more expensive.

Year					Year			
Month	Rain Fall	Temperature Max	Temperature Min	Comments	Month	Rain Fall	Temperature Max	Temperature Min
Jan					Jan			
Feb					Feb			
Mar					Mar			
April					April			
May					May			
June					June			
July					July			
Aug					Aug			
Sept					Sept			
Oct					Oct			
Nov					Nov			
Dec					Dec			

Weather Worries

SNOW
Don't worry. On the ground it acts as a warm, dry blanket for low-growing plants.
Only on the branches of evergreen trees and shrubs can it do damage – snapping them
as it thaws. Knock it off before it can do any harm.

FROST
Keep off frosted grass. Walk over it and you'll discover brown footprints when the
warmer weather comes. Grow really tender shrubs against house walls for protection.
Alternatively, lag tender plants with straw held in place with plastic netting.

WIND
Strong winds have a drying effect on plants. Protect newly-planted shrubs on windy
sites by surrounding them with a screen made of sacking, or with a tube made from an old
plastic compost or fertilizer sack. Stake floppy plants before they reach toppling height.
Use twiggy branches, or circles of stiff wire on legs.

DROUGHT
Don't wait until plants are crisp before watering, and don't simply dampen the
surface of the soil. Check with a trowel to see how far down the soil is dry. If it's dry
more than an inch below the surface, switch on a garden sprinkler for 2 hours. You don't
have to wait until evening to water; do the job when you have the time.

COMMENTS	YEAR				COMMENTS
	MONTH	RAIN FALL	TEMPERATURE MAX	MIN	
	JAN				
	FEB				
	MAR				
	APRIL				
	MAY				
	JUNE				
	JULY				
	AUG				
	SEPT				
	OCT				
	NOV				
	DEC				

The Flower Garden

I suppose it smacks rather of the Victorian era to talk about 'The Flower Garden' as though it were some walled paradise where you could escape the daily bustle and wander at leisure among fragrant blooms. But most gardeners do still think in terms of the largest part of their plot being devoted to flowers, even if these are best seen when planted among trees and shrubs.

Aside from these woody giants, the longest-lasting of the flowers are those called herbaceous perennials. It's a nasty name for a lovely group of plants which, once bought, will die down every winter but re-emerge in spring, hopefully larger than ever before. Call them 'border plants' if you hate the other mouthful; they really are the stalwart bloomers in any garden and grow for the laziest owners.

Most rock plants are perennials, too. They are smaller, demand brilliant drainage and full sun in most cases, and as well as being used on rock gardens (or those heaps of stones and dusty earth known as 'rockeries') they are useful chaps for the front of beds and borders where they can spill on to paths (and on to lawns to make mowing difficult!).

Among these permanent inhabitants of the garden you can grow the temporary occupants – those plants with shorter lives that are known as annuals. One year is all they last, but what a show they make. There are the hardy annuals that are happy to be sown direct in the garden in all but the heaviest soils during March and April, to bloom where they were scattered. Then there are the half-hardy annuals. These are the bedding plants sold by nurseries and greengrocers in May for summer flowers. They have to be sown under glass in early spring, pricked out into trays and allowed to grow larger before being planted in the garden when all danger of frost is past. Of all garden flowers, the half-hardy annuals tend to be the most generous with their blooms.

Just to complicate matters, there are plants called biennials that are sown one year to flower the next. Wallflowers are treated as biennials (even though they are truly perennial if left to grow on after blooming). Sweet williams and those all-too-infrequently-seen Canterbury bells are true biennials. All are sown in the spring of one year to bloom in the spring of the next year.

The best way of growing all these flowers is to have drifts and pockets of different kinds in different parts of the garden. Leave patches of earth for the temporary annuals among larger drifts of permanent border plants. And have an eye for form and texture as well as colour. It's fun to see a squat, round-leafed plant next to one that has a vertical forest of sword-shaped foliage, or a fussy, cut-leafed plant against one with huge, rubbery leaves. Invent your own schemes – it's the best part of gardening.

If you're a born coward where colour is concerned, you can always resort to a single-colour border. A white border; a red border, or a blue border. Remember always to have plenty of green in the scheme to avoid monotony.

The biggest headache of all is plant spacing. With trees and shrubs it's sensible to space them so they have room to grow undisturbed to their full size, even if this will take them five or ten years. It's no fun adopting this principle with other flowers. Plant thickly if you can afford it; that way weeds will be smothered before they have a chance to establish themselves, and your plants will really seem to enjoy one another's company.

Choose the right plant for the right part of your garden. There are those that enjoy shade and those that relish full sun; those that can tolerate dry soil and those that grow strongly in heavy, moist earth.

And finally, remember that even border plants have striking foliage that lasts far longer than the blooms. Look for it and use it to your advantage.

Flower Garden Plans

Here's the place to start planning your new beds and borders. Mark out their precise dimensions, then plot in the plants, taking into account their colour, shape, form, texture and eventual size. Give the shrubs, trees and roses that like to grow undisturbed plenty of room to stretch to their full size. The border plants, annuals and bulbs that go between them can be more closely planted and thinned out later as their bedfellows start to bully them. That way you'll never have a sparse-looking garden.

Write the name of each plant over its symbol, rather than numbering the symbol and having a key. It's so much easier to visualize a planting if you don't have to cross-refer. Blobs of colour brushed on to each plant will show you the colour pattern of your patchwork, but remember that not all plants flower at the same time.

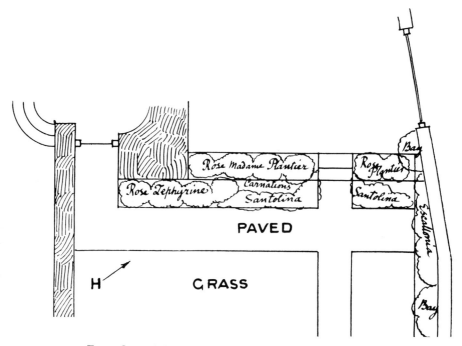

From: Gertrude Jekyll, *Gardens for Small Country Houses* (1912)

'I work with nature, not against it, and use only plants that will thrive in my area.'
Sir Frederick Gibberd, *The Englishman's Garden* (1982)

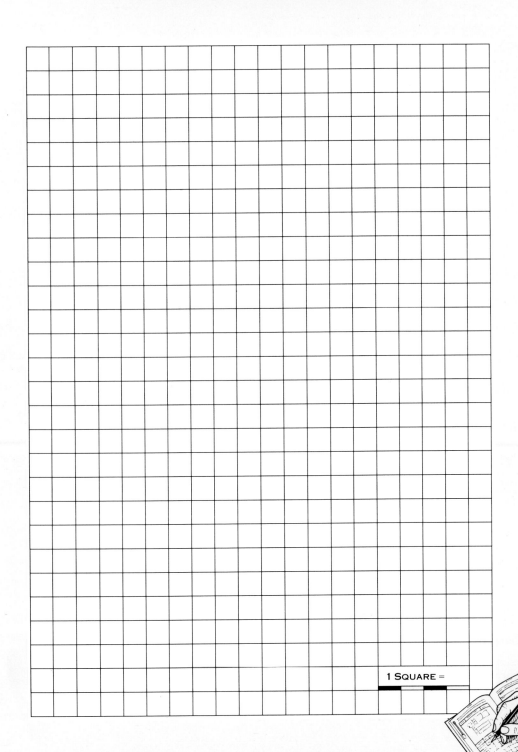

1 SQUARE =

Flower Garden Plans

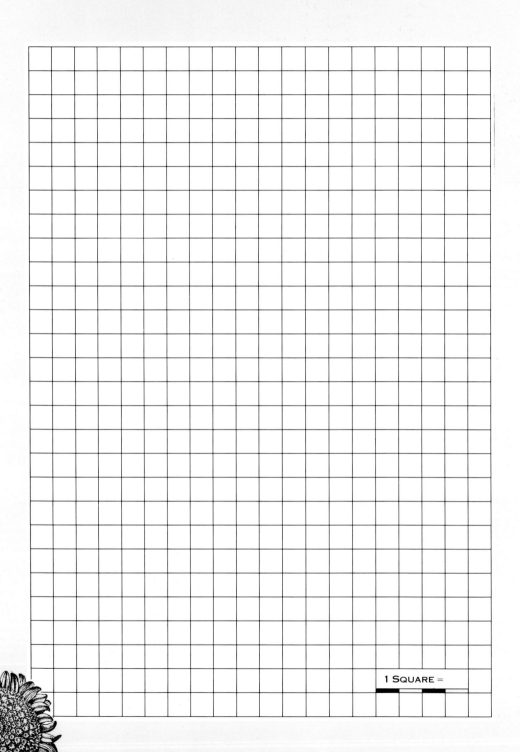

1 SQUARE =

'The most important thing is to clothe the garden with thick planting. One must be brave and ignore the statutory rules about distance between plants – they are traditional head-gardener's rules and date back to bedding days – and plant more closely, feeding the soil well so that it can support a denser population.'
Anne Scott-James, *Down to Earth* (1971)

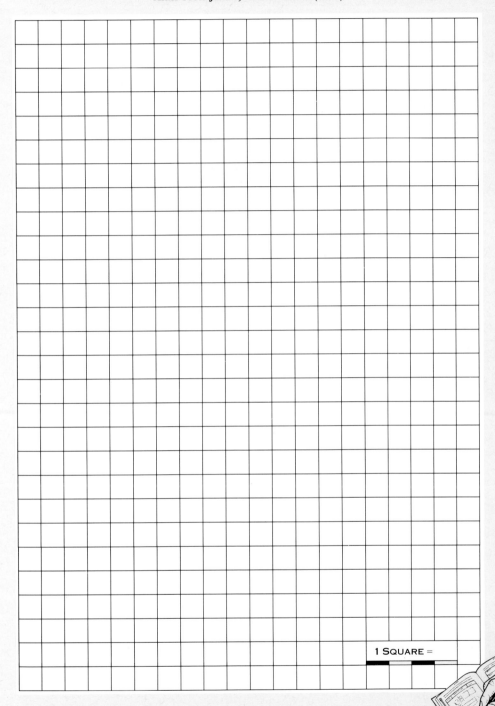

1 SQUARE =

Flower Garden Notebook

'Sometimes, in summer, I imagine I could fill up pages without drawing breath, I have so much to say about the way a newly planted area is filling up, or what a fool I have been to have planted something in past years which now I have a battle to eradicate. My worry at the moment is where to begin.'

Beth Chatto, *The Dry Garden* (1978)

PLANT NAME	SITE	PROBLEM	MOVE TO	AVAILABLE FROM

Make notes of any plants in your garden that are obviously in the wrong place,
and plants in other people's gardens that you long to acquire. And remember: it often pays
to move a plant to its new site as soon as you spot the place for it, even if that means
uprooting it in the middle of summer. Given plenty of water in the first couple of weeks the
chances are that it will soon settle in.

PLANT NAME	SITE	PROBLEM	MOVE TO	AVAILABLE FROM

The Bulb Plan

I've labelled clumps of bulbs till I'm blue in the face, but as I'm no match for my two small daughters or the army of blackbirds that enjoys hauling the tags from the soil, it's much easier to make a map. Use this grid to plot the buried treasure in your garden and with any luck you'll be able to find the bulbs when you want to move them, and to avoid them when you plant something else.

Draw in the shapes of beds and borders; mark the shape of each drift of bulbs and number it. Identify the bulb in the key below.

1 15 CROCUS BOT. - mixed	21
2 15 CHONODOXA LUC. Blue	22
3 15 ALLIUM OSTROWKIANUM - purple	23
4 15 TUL·PRAESTANS TUBV -RED	24
5	25
6	26
7	27
8	28
9	29
10	30
11	31
12	32
13	33
14	34
15	35
16	36
17	37
18	38
19	39
20	40

'Adequate labelling of bulbs is more essential than for any other class of plant, otherwise one
is entirely at sea at planting or lifting time.'
E.B. Anderson, *Dwarf Bulbs for the Rock Garden* (1959)

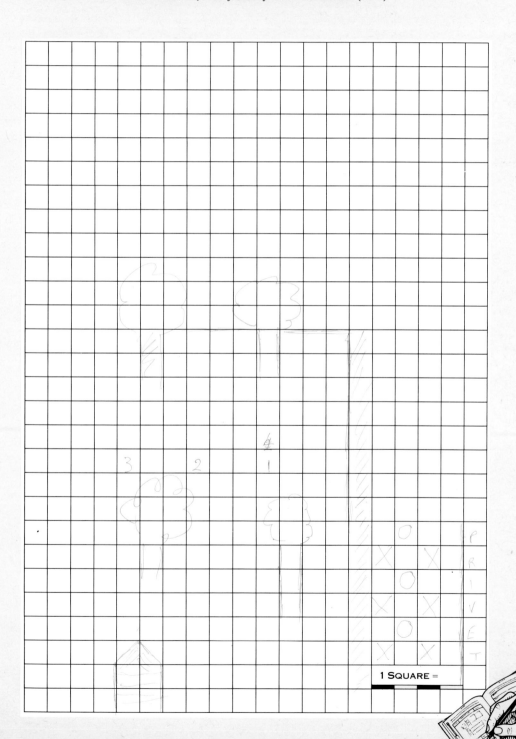

1 SQUARE =

Roses

The flowers that dreams are made on. I know of one or two gardeners who won't grow them because of their thorns, but no-one with an ounce of feeling could deny their beauty or do without their scents. Asking someone if he likes roses is rather like asking if he likes music; there are so many different sorts that at least one is bound to appeal.

Gardeners with miniscule plots can grow the miniature roses in pots and tubs and even window-boxes. On plants only a foot high they'll carry perfectly formed roses right through the summer.

The real enthusiasts for bedding will stand by their hybrid teas and floribundas – the first fat and cabbage-like, the second with clusters of slightly smaller flowers carried in far greater number. Both can possess heady scents and prove that modern roses still fill the air with fragrance.

But the connoisseur of scents, and the gardener with an eye for fashion, will always turn to the shrub rose. Large or small it has an unrestrained habit, and probably a shorter flowering season than the bushy hybrid teas and floribundas, but it makes up for that with a plenitude of blossom in its season and a powerful perfume. Choose the modern varieties of shrub rose and you can rely on a longer season of flowering, too.

For walls and posts and pergolas and arches there are the climbers and the ramblers, and these last named look especially good when growing up through a tree – an old apple that's past its best, or a boring green-leaved tree that needs brightening up in summer.

Don't think of roses as something for beds where they are grown alone; they relish the company of other plants and look far better for it, too. Who wants to be lumbered with a patch of bare earth below the roses where weeds can colonize to their heart's content? The roses certainly won't enjoy being prodded among every few days – you'll only produce a forest of suckers for your trouble. No; give them some legitimate company. Either plant them as shrubs among other border flowers, or if you prefer to grow them in a bed of their own then do so, but underplant them with violets or hardy geraniums; edge the bed with lavender or catmint or pinks; you'll improve the display and cut down the work.

Whichever roses you grow, they'll all appreciate a nourishing bit of soil. Manure and compost are mother's milk to them, so don't stint on the organic enrichment. They'll simply sit and sulk in poor, dry earth.

And then there's the pruning. It's really not as complicated as you might think. It's a job best done between January and March, whatever the type of rose. Use a sharp pair of secateurs and approach your bush with courage. Hybrid teas and floribundas are reduced to about knee height. Try to make an open-centred, cup-shaped framework of young, vigorous branches. Cut out completely any branches that are dead, diseased or weak, and one or two of the old, gnarled ones. When you cut back the rest to knee height, make each cut just above an outward-facing bud. That's all there is to it with the bushes.

Shrub roses are easier to tackle. Just snip out any dead bits and then thin the framework of branches by removing one or two overcrowding and aged stems each year. Don't, as a rule, cut any of them back; instead cut them out completely. That way you'll retain the natural shape of the shrub.

Miniatures can be pruned in the same way as hybrid teas and floribundas, but they won't really make it as high as your knee so reduce them by one third of their height.

Climbers and ramblers are the trickiest. If I were you I'd simply snip back their sideshoots to three buds every winter, and remove the occasional long stem when it really looks past it. Nothing like an easy way out!

Finally, the pests and diseases. All this work could put you off growing roses for life, but rest assured that one or two good 'cocktail' sprays of a combined insecticide and fungicide at the very start of the growing season (in April and May) will help to keep your roses in the peak of health for the rest of the season. That, and a couple of feeds with rose fertilizer (once in April and once in June), plus a good mulch of manure in spring are really all that's necessary. Honest!

Rose Garden Plan

If your roses grow neatly (or rampantly) all together in a bed, draw the bed or border shape here and plot in the varieties. If you're a lover of roses in all parts of the garden your plan will have to be larger, and perhaps simple crosses must suffice to mark the location of each rose. Don't shirk from doing this; labels fade and disappear, even when securely fastened to the stem of the rose. Somehow it's always the labelled stem that's cut at pruning time!

1	21
2	22
3	23
4	24
5	25
6	26
7	27
8	28
9	29
10	30
11	31
12	32
13	33
14	34
15	35
16	36
17	37
18	38
19	39
20	40

'Gather ye rosebuds while ye may
Old Time is still a-flying,
And that same flower that blooms today,
Tomorrow may be dying.'
Robert Herrick, *Hesperides* (1648)

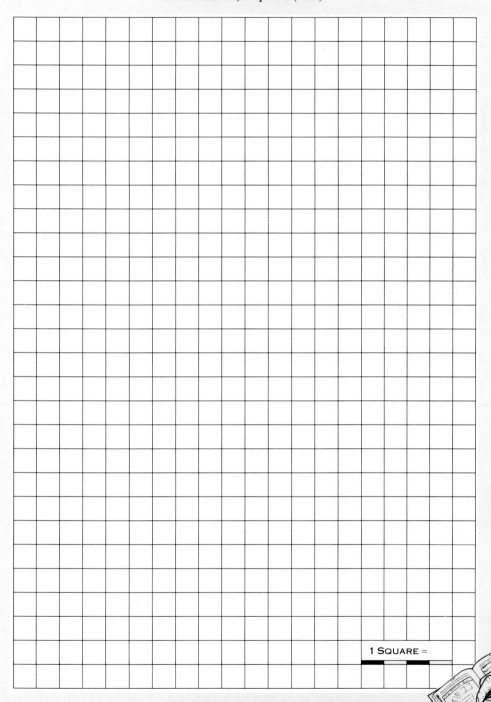

1 SQUARE =

Rose Records

Keep a record of the performance of your roses and you'll soon spot the ones that are the best 'doers' in your garden. Jot down the names of varieties seen in other gardens, too, and order them well in time for autumn planting.

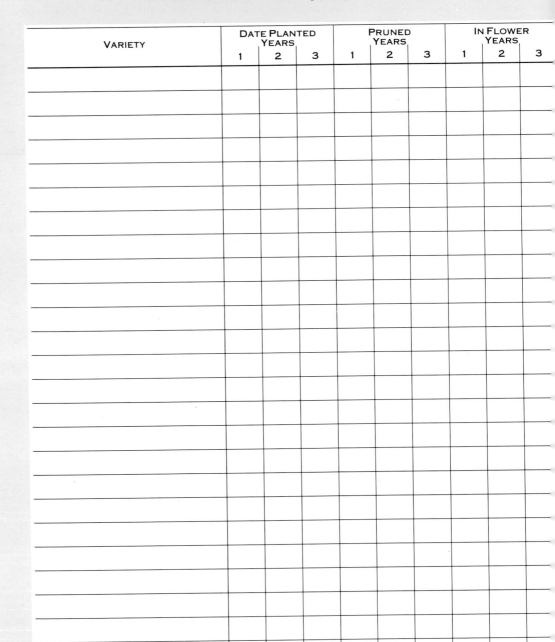

VARIETY	DATE PLANTED YEARS			PRUNED YEARS			IN FLOWER YEARS		
	1	2	3	1	2	3	1	2	3

'When going back to school in September, I used to take with me a pointed flower of Souvenir de la Malmaison, packed in an empty barley-sugar tin; it kept fresh in that tin box for a long time, and daily I would take it out, admire it and recall happy memories of home of which it reminded me.'

The Rev. Joseph H. Pemberton
Roses: Their History, Development and Cultivation (1920)

FRAGRANCE	HEALTHY?	SPRAYS USED (INCLUDING DATES)	REMARKS

Trees and Shrubs

The phrase you'll hear quoted more than any other about trees and shrubs is that they are 'the backbone of the garden'. And so they are. The problem is that in a tiny garden you'll only have room for a tiny backbone. No matter. Make good use of a handful of bold shrubs and maybe one small tree as a focal point (another favourite phrase) and you'll see that the experts are absolutely right – these meaty plants provide a boldness of form that gives any plot stature.

It makes sense to avoid planting really hefty trees – willows in particular – right next to the house. They'll shift your foundations with amazing ease. Willows are for very large gardens, and no tree should be nearer than fifteen feet from your house walls. Shrubs are not nearly so troublesome and you can plant them, along with climbers, right up to the house so that it's enveloped by the garden.

There's a great temptation to fill a garden with flowering shrubs: fragrant mock-orange blossom, lilac, weigela and deutzia. They're all a delight in their season, but what a short season it is. No; start off by positioning your tree, or trees, and then plot in some plants to provide permanent shape – evergreen shrubs.

Evergreens are invaluable, for they give the garden year-round form and texture and colour. It's all beginning to sound a little Christian Dior, but however untrained your eye it *does* notice things like foliage textures as well as a brilliant splash of scarlet bedding in summer. Don't overdo the evergreens, mind; unless you enjoy an unchanging landscape reminiscent of a cemetery. And remember that many evergreens are really evergolds, everyellows, everblues and evervariegateds. Ring the changes.

Once your evergreens are in place, then you can fill in with a few flowering shrubs, making sure they're in a position where they can be admired in their season of glory, but where they won't be a prominent bore when simply in leaf.

And what about planting distances? Give shrubs room to develop happily to their final size. Nurserymen's catalogues will usually tell you what that is and you should allow for it. Fill in the gaps meanwhile with border plants and the like – unless you're feeling energetic and extravagant. If you are, then plant your shrubs more closely and be prepared to move them when they outgrow their spot. There are few rules in gardening, and if breaking them gives you pleasure, break away.

One thing you can't stint on is soil preparation. Do it well. Generally trees and shrubs are the longest-lived inhabitants of the garden and it makes sense to put as much organic enrichment beneath them as you can.

Shrubs won't need staking, but some trees will. Dig the hole, work in the enrichment, knock in the stake, plant the tree, replace the soil, firm it, mulch it and tie tree to stake with two ties. The top of the stake should finish just below the lowest branch. That's all there is to it. However, there are those who say that trees don't need to be staked except in the most exposed places. Take a chance if you want, and hope that your children don't swing from the trunk before it's fattened up.

As to the planting season, bare-root trees and shrubs are committed to the earth between November and March; container-grown plants at any time of year provided the earth is neither dusty dry, frozen solid or soggy mud. I'd plump for container-grown plants if I were you; they always seem to get away better than rudely interrupted plants that have been prised unwillingly from nursery rows.

Oh, and one final word: water. Trees and shrubs in their first year of establishment need lots of it, so be ready with the buckets in dry weather.

Tree and Shrub Records

The trees and larger specimen shrubs you plant in your garden are worth recording individually. They are unlikely to be very cheap, and it's worth taking a bit of extra care over their welfare.

PLANT NAME	COST	DATE PLANTED	DATE PRUNED	DATE FED	LOCATION	REMARKS

'A tree that has been well looked after from its infancy will show a vigour both in girth and height over neglected trees that will be a surprise to many, and a good object-lesson to those who think that everything may be left to nature.'

Canon Ellacombe, *In A Gloucestershire Garden* (1895)

PLANT NAME	COST	DATE PLANTED	DATE PRUNED	DATE FED	LOCATION	REMARKS

Tree and Shrub Calendar

Jot down the trees and shrubs that make impact in your garden, and indicate on the right hand page the times at which that impact is most enjoyed. At the end of each year you'll be able to see at a glance when blooms and leaf effects are thin on the ground. It's a simple matter then to take one of those exciting trips to the garden centre or nursery; to spot a plant that cheers and to bring it home and tuck it in.

PLANT NAME	FLOWER	LEAF	FRUIT	STEM

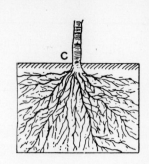

'Gardener, if you listen, listen well:
Plant for your winter pleasure, when the months
Dishearten; plant to find a fragile note
Touched from the brittle violin of frost.'
Vita Sackville-West, *The Garden* (1946)

JAN	FEB	MAR	APRIL	MAY	JUNE	JULY	AUG	SEPT	OCT	NOV	DEC

Growing Your Own

You can buy plants and plant 'em and enjoy 'em. But compare that enjoyment with the pleasure derived from growing a plant from a seed, or a cutting, or a bit you were given from a plant owned by the lady down the road, and you'll find that there's a world of difference.

Propagation, they say, is the purest of human pleasures. There can be no denying that. Most folk know how to sow a seed in the garden; for summer flowers, hardy annuals can be scattered on all but the stickiest soil in April, lightly raked in and allowed to grow where they emerge. A little thinning out of overcrowded seedlings may be all that is necessary to ensure a bright display.

There are pitfalls, though. Some gardeners will sow too deeply (a common fault); others will sow in cold, sticky earth and their seeds will simply rot; yet more will allow the seeds to dry out. Don't fall into any of these traps and you'll succeed with seeds. They want to be buried to just twice their own depth in warm, moist soil that doesn't dry out, and then they'll do well.

But annuals are not the only plants to grow from seeds. Border plants that are perennial can also be grown very cheaply this way if you've a little patience. Sown like bedding plants under glass in spring; pricked out into trays and then planted out in rows on a spare patch of ground, they'll have reached flowering size one year later and will save you pounds. It's sad that few gardeners seem to know about this method of growing lupins and delphiniums and all manner of traditional border plants. Or is it just that they'd rather buy a potful for instant flowers?

You'll need a fraction more patience to raise shrubs and trees from seeds, but it can still be done, and without any heat at that. A cold frame in the garden into which the pots of seeds can be placed is all that's needed. It's not so much the heat that these plants require to get them to grow, more the protection that the frame provides from slugs, insects, wayward feet and weeds.

Sowing times for trees and shrubs vary. Some seeds need to be sown in autumn and frozen during the winter after sowing to shock them into growth; others swell happily as soon as they are sown in spring and grow like mustard and cress. Specialist firms sell the seeds and will also offer advice in the form of pertinent notes on the back of the packet.

When you've a spare moment in between all these spring sowings, get out with a spade and chop up your border plants. The overcrowded ones, that is. Most of them prefer to be divided into smaller clumps every three years or so (except stick-in-the-muds like peonies which prefer to sit undisturbed). Dig up the clump and slice it into smaller pieces slightly larger than your clenched fist. Replant these immediately and they'll grow away well. Only the dead centre of the old clump need be discarded.

I recommend spring for dividing plants simply because my own soil is on the sticky side. If you've sandy earth, as I had in my last garden, you'll find that autumn division is far better. Drainage is good through the winter and the plants will fatten up well, producing far larger, more floriferous clumps in their first year than if they were divided in spring.

But I suppose the operation that gives the most satisfaction is the taking of cuttings. At any time between May and July, many shrubs are producing healthy shoots that can be cut off, trimmed to around three inches long by cutting just under a leaf joint, stripped of all but their topmost pair of leaves and rooted on a windowsill in a pot of peat and sand covered with a polythene bag. Some house plants like African violets can even be rooted from leaves plonked in jars of water. The temptation to take cuttings is irresistible.

Not all of them need heat, neither do they need to be taken in summer and cossetted in dry weather. Rose shoots ten inches long and as thick as a pencil can be cut from bushes in September (cut neatly below a leaf at the base and above a leaf at the top) and all but the top two leaves pulled off. Then bury the cuttings in a sand-lined trench in the garden so that just the top three inches of stem protrudes. They'll root and grow away during the following summer and can be transplanted in autumn to their permanent positions. Magic, I call it.

Lawn Care Calendar

People worry about lawns. They want them to look like bowling greens and yet demand no more attention than a bit of carpet. It's an impossible compromise. If you want a hard-wearing yet verdant greensward you'll have to lay the right turf or sow the right seed – one with *dwarf* ryegrasses in it that wear well and yet do not stand up too high and so refuse to be cut by the mower.

When your lawn is established it will need regular attention. Here's what you can do and when:

JANUARY
Keep off the grass, except to rake up leaves. Have the mower serviced.

ᵥ **FEBRUARY**
Lay turf if the ground is not frozen or muddy (it's a job you can do during any month with a ᵥ against it).

ᵥ **MARCH**
Late in the month, give the lawn its first mow – a light one.

ᵥ **APRIL**
Kill moss. Apply a weed and feed mixture late in the month. Continue mowing from now on as often as is necessary.

ᵥ **MAY**
A good month for killing lawn weeds. Mow once a week. Sow new lawns.

JUNE
Water the lawn in prolonged dry spells. Mow twice weekly.

JULY
Feed the lawn if you're feeling generous. Keep mowing.

AUGUST
Your last chance to feed with any fertilizer designed to green-up the lawn. Still keep on mowing.

SEPTEMBER
Second chance to sow new lawns. Scarify the lawn (rake it to remove dead grass), spike it (to improve drainage), and, if you're really keen, topdress it with loam, peat and sand.

ᵥ **OCTOBER**
Repair broken edges. Ease off mowing.

ᵥ**NOVEMBER**
Rake up leaves; store and clean the mower.

ᵥ **DECEMBER**
Rest.

Lawn Diary

'Why, oh! why, will people cut up their lawns and fill them with horrid little beds?'
Margery Fish, *We Made A Garden* (1956)

Whether you're an ardent lawn manicurist, or simply the 'quick wash and brush up' type,
you might find it useful to take notes of what you did to your lawn and when. Even the
roughest grass can be turned into a smart patch of greensward with an occasional weed and
feed. Use one chart for each lawn or each year.

	DATES				
FIRST MOWED	20 Sept 93				
FED					
KILLED WEEDS					
WEED/FEED					
WORMS KILLED					
PATCHED					
SPIKED					
SCARIFIED					
ROLLED					
TOP DRESSED					
WATERED					
EDGES RE-CUT					
OTHER TREATMENT					

LAWN HISTORY
Did you sow it, turf it or discover it? If the latter; what state was it in?

Lawn Diary

'There is no more distressing situation in the whole of gardening than to watch a lawn
deteriorate to the point where it is an ugly eyesore, a patchwork quilt of greens and browns.
And it is so unnecessary, for Britain is the home of the Beautiful Lawn.'
Dr D.G. Hessayon, *The Lawn Expert* (1982)

	DATES				
FIRST MOWED					
FED					
KILLED WEEDS					
WEED/FEED					
WORMS KILLED					
PATCHED					
SPIKED					
SCARIFIED					
ROLLED					
TOP DRESSED					
WATERED					
EDGES RE-CUT					
OTHER TREATMENT					

Lawn Diary

'Avant-gardeners do not have lawns; they have grass. But not much. The "bowling green" lawn is a feature that belongs in front of council houses where it is surrounded by borders of lobelia, alyssum, French marigolds and salvias with standard fuchsias used as "dot plants".'
Alan Titchmarsh, *Avant-Gardening:*
A Guide to One-Upmanship in the Garden (1984)

	DATES					
FIRST MOWED						
FED						
KILLED WEEDS						
WEED/FEED						
WORMS KILLED						
PATCHED						
SPIKED						
SCARIFIED						
ROLLED						
TOP DRESSED						
WATERED						
EDGES RE-CUT						
OTHER TREATMENT						

Crop Protection

Without going to ridiculous lengths or extravagant expense you can steal a march on nature both at the beginning and the end of the season by a quick cover-up. Donkey's years ago, gardeners used glass domes known as bell jars to protect their crops from the ravages of the weather. Sadly these ornamental artefacts are now things of the past, but at least their modern counterparts are not so fragile. The name 'cloche' still persists in relation to almost every kind of plant covering and acts as a permanent reminder of the origins of these mini-greenhouses.

Start to use cloches on the vegetable plot in the New Year, placing them over ground where early crops are to be sown. They'll protect the earth from the worst of the weather so that it warms up in advance of the surrounding soil. Once the crop is sown it will be sheltered from chilling winds and lashing rain, so that as well as having earlier crops you'll have clean ones, too.

The cheapest 'cloches' are polythene tunnels made from plastic sheeting stretched taut over wire hoops and held in place with nylon twine. Flashier models are of rigid plastic and contain ventilation panels that can be opened and closed as dictated by the weather. Whatever the material the cloches can be used at the end of the season as well as the beginning. They'll help outdoor tomatoes to continue ripening; they'll keep your onions dry after lifting, and they'll even stop Christmas roses – *Helleborus niger* – from being splashed by mud.

Lately gardeners have seen further developments in the use of plastics for crop forcing. There's now an assortment of sheeting on the market – some of it clear, some of it opaque, some of it fibrous and some of it perforated – which can be laid flat on the soil after the crop has been sown. As germination takes place below it, the sheet retains warmth and moisture, making it easier for the crop to grow until it is large enough to be uncovered and allowed to fend for itself.

But for the gardener who wants a cheap greenhouse, to raise bedding plants in spring or to overwinter a few geraniums and fuchsias, the frame's the thing. Buy one if you must, but it's almost as easy to make one at home from an old window frame laid on top of a wooden or brick box. Just like that it will enable you to grow early flower or vegetable seedlings. If, however, you can provide heat in the form of soil- and air-warming cables it becomes much more versatile and will enable you to prolong even further the season of food production in a small garden. Try it and see!

Greenhouse Gardening

Are you really committed to this gardening lark? Do you feel a sense of deep pleasure when ministering to your plants? Are you quite prepared to look after a select bunch of them every day of the year? If the answer to all three questions is 'yes', then go ahead and buy a greenhouse. If you're a 'don't know', then don't.

There's as much responsibility attached to owning a greenhouse as there is to owning a dog or a cat, though the hours that the greenhouse demands will often be far in excess of the time craved by a dumb friend. Am I putting you off? I don't mean to. For if you're happy to work with your plants at all times of year you'll have a whale of a time under cover.

Think carefully before you buy your greenhouse. Should it be wooden or aluminium? Both are good, so it's simply a matter of taste and of whether you are prepared to apply a preservative to the timber model every couple of years. Do you want a free-standing model or one that is attached to the house wall? The latter will have lower fuel bills and be easy of access if it can be entered directly from the house.

What do you want to grow? If you're thinking in terms of tomatoes and cucumbers you'll need a greenhouse that's glazed to ground level, but if pot plants are more your forte then a half-timbered model will mask that unsightly space below the staging and give better insulation, too.

Whichever style you decide on, go for the largest size you can fit in. The greenhouse may look enormous when it comes, but you'll soon fill it to bursting, and the more room that's available for raising your own bedding plants, vegetables and the like, the more money you'll save.

As soon as it's in place you'll find yourself tempted by a hundred-and-one gadgets that are supposed to make the growing easier. Select carefully. If I had to choose just one gadget for my greenhouse, it would be an automatic ventilating arm. These natty little devices can be attached to the ventilators and set to open and close them at pre-set temperatures. If you're out for the day they'll cope with that unexpected burst of sunshine that would otherwise have fried your seedlings in your absence.

Will your greenhouse be heated or not? It's a big decision, and often a costly one. It's possible to save quite a lot of money with an unheated greenhouse, and to raise a good number of plants and crops early in the season, but a little heat does make your structure even more valuable. You'll have to decide for yourself what you can afford, but I have to say that I find electricity by far the best bet.

I used to use paraffin. It was cheaper then, but it had (and still has) two big disadvantages: it produces fumes, and it produces copious amounts of water in winter, both of which some of your plants may find offensive. What's more, there's no way of controlling a paraffin heater thermostatically. Now I use electric tubular heaters linked to a thermostat set at around 45°F (7°C). It keeps the frost out in winter, it's clean and dry and I hardly notice a difference in my electricity bill.

When moist air is desirable – usually in spring and summer – it's a good idea to damp down the floor of the greenhouse (simply water it with a hosepipe or water can). A flagstone path down the middle will make access easy, but I find that gravel is cheaper, neat and easy to lay, and it holds on to the moisture for rather longer than a hard surface.

When it comes to staging, make sure the stuff is well built. Moist pot plants weigh more than you'd think and it's heartbreaking if your Heath Robinson shelving comes crashing down under the weight of all your home-grown summer bedding. Oh, and one last thing. When you build your greenhouse, make sure it's sitting on sturdy foundations, and that it's well anchored to them. If it's not, you're likely to find it sitting upside-down in next-door's garden after the first gale of autumn.

Do you still want a greenhouse? Of course you do!

Greenhouse Propagation Records

Nothing is more infuriating than to forget how long ago a particular pot of seeds was sown
(so you don't know when you can legitimately give up hope), or when a plant was last potted
on to give it a boost.
Record your seed sowings and pottings-up, your hits and your misses to guard against
repeated failures in future years, and to cash in on the successes.

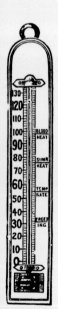

VARIETY	SOWN/ CUTTINGS TAKEN	TREATMENT	GERMINATION	PRICKED OFF	POTTED

'The briefness of the British summer and the frequent interruptions to out-door enjoyment, occasioned by adverse weather, render the well-kept plant house a place of most agreeable resort at every season of the year.'
Shirley Hibberd, *The Amateur's Greenhouse and Conservatory* (1880)

POT SIZE	COMPOST	PLANTED OUT	OTHER TREATMENT	PERFORMANCE

Greenhouse Propagation Records

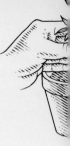

Variety	Sown/ Cuttings Taken	Treatment	Germination	Pricked Off	Potted

'First he ate some lettuces and some French beans; and then he ate some radishes; and then,
feeling rather sick, he went to look for some parsley.
But round the end of a cucumber frame, whom should he meet but Mr McGregor!'
Beatrix Potter, *The Tale of Peter Rabbit* (1902)

POT SIZE	COMPOST	PLANTED OUT	OTHER TREATMENT	PERFORMANCE

Greenhouse Hygiene Records

You'll find that some plants don't much like washing-up water laced with today's detergents, and in the greenhouse (where the humid environment helps them to multiply faster than rabbits), greenflies, whiteflies, red spider mites and the like really have to be kept in check on a regular basis.
There are suggestions of appropriate chemicals on page 104; keep notes here of what you spray and when.

PROBLEM	DATE	PLANTS AFFECTED	TREATMENT	REMARKS

'In the days when the family laundry was done in a kitchen tub with strong yellow soap,
washing water was a popular pesticide, particularly used for the white cottage garden lilies.'
Margaret Baker, *The Gardener's Folklore* (1977)

PROBLEM	DATE	PLANTS AFFECTED	TREATMENT	REMARKS

Greenhouse Crop Records

Individual greenhouse crops such as vines, peaches, cucumbers, melons and tomatoes deserve a bit of special attention. Record the varieties you grow and their performance.

VARIETY	SOWN/ PLANTED	POTTED	COMPOST	PLANTED OUT	PRUNED	FED

'He was in charge of the Royal Garden fruit houses which comprised greenhouses for cucumbers, melons and strawberries together with two fruit ranges, each a quarter of a mile long which, divided into four, served the four seasons of the year.'
Percy Thrower on the fruit foreman at Windsor, in *My Lifetime of Gardening* (1977)

SPRAYED	OTHER TREATMENT	HARVESTED	COMMENTS

Greenhouse Crop Records

'Of all the fruits, in my opinion, a freshly gathered ripe apricot is the finest fruit of all.'
Fred Loads, *Gardening Tips of a Lifetime* (1980)

VARIETY	SOWN/ PLANTED	POTTED	COMPOST	PLANTED OUT	PRUNED	FED

'If yer want yer grape voine ter grow strong, yer've got ter dig a big hole before yer plant it
and put in the bottom tree dead dogs.'
Unknown Irishman to the author

SPRAYED	OTHER TREATMENT	HARVESTED	COMMENTS

The Vegetable Garden

They say you can tell people's characters simply by looking at their gardens. You can tell even more about them, I reckon, by looking at their vegetable plots. And I don't just mean whether or not they like spinach.

Of course, the crops a person grows say quite a bit about his mealtime preferences. Or they should do. The trouble is that many gardeners have to grow certain vegetables just to please other members of the family; you'd be surprised how many vegetable growers dislike half the produce on their plot.

Likes and dislikes apart, it's your method of growing vegetables that gives you away. Most folk will arrange their crops in long, straight rows; the more the grower is a perfectionist, the straighter the rows. It's a technique that's been tried and tested over the years and it makes sense to carry on with it – straight rows are easy to hoe between and easy to sow. But they have their disadvantages, too. How many times have you sown a complete row just for the sake of neatness, only to find that you've been presented with a tremendous, unusable glut at the end of the season? What a waste.

Far better to sow a third of a row every two or three weeks, so spreading the maturity of the crop over a longer period of time. Alternatively, give up sowing in straight rows and start sowing in patches.

This technique is a really good idea where the vegetable plot is a part of a garden that must be good-looking as well as productive. Instead of marking out rows on your veg patch, divide it into three-foot wide beds with 1½-foot paths between to allow for access. The long beds can, in turn, be divided into smaller units anything from three feet long upwards, to accommodate the individual crops.

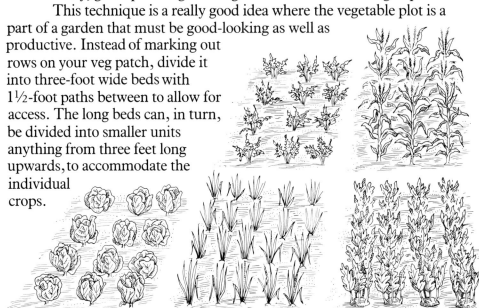

Make each bed four feet long and you'll be able to stitch a sort of vegetable patchwork quilt that makes edible bedding. Plan your patchwork vegetable garden so that the foliage of one crop shows off that of another – carrots against beetroot; Swiss chard against Salad Bowl lettuce; leeks against red-leafed lettuce – and you'll be the envy of your neighbours.

What's more this scheme makes weeding and other cultivations much less of an ordeal. Psychologically it's far easier to tackle one three-foot by four-foot bed at a time than it is to approach a twenty-foot row. You're less likely to be bored by a monotonous diet, too, if you make sure you have plenty of squares, each one packed with a different crop.

If your garden is really small, don't rule out vegetables altogether. Instead, grow them in your flowerbeds and borders. Chard, beetroot, carrots, lettuces, leeks, onions, parsley and lots more vegetables are excellent foliage plants. The only problem is bringing yourself to cut them when they reach maturity!

Vegetable Plotting

You'll save yourself the trouble of digging in surpluses, with any luck, if you make a cropping plan before you sow or plant. With a seed catalogue or the packets themselves by your side, work out which crop should go where; when to sow it and how much you need. The space-saving wheezes shown on page 76 should also be a help.

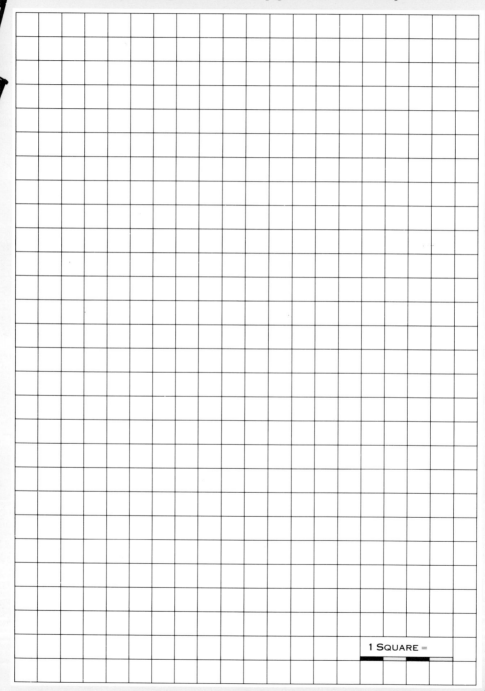

1 SQUARE =

'There need be no fallowing – no resting of the ground, and if it should so happen that by hard cropping perplexity arises about the disposal of produce, the proverbial three courses are open – to sell, to give, or to dig the stuff in as manure.'
Sutton & Sons, *The Culture of Vegetables and Flowers* (1895)

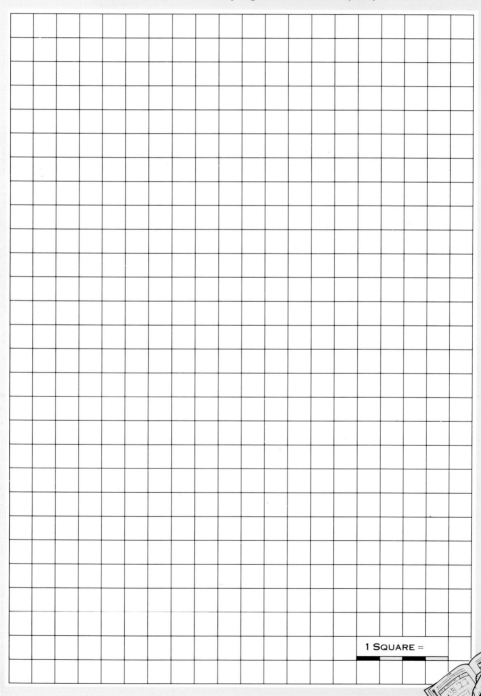

1 SQUARE =

Vegetable Plotting

'Most folk seem to turn into millionaires once they get a packet of seeds in their hands. They
sow so lavishly that the poor little things can't germinate and get choked in the rush. So
remember never to pour your seeds straight from the packet into the bed; you can't control

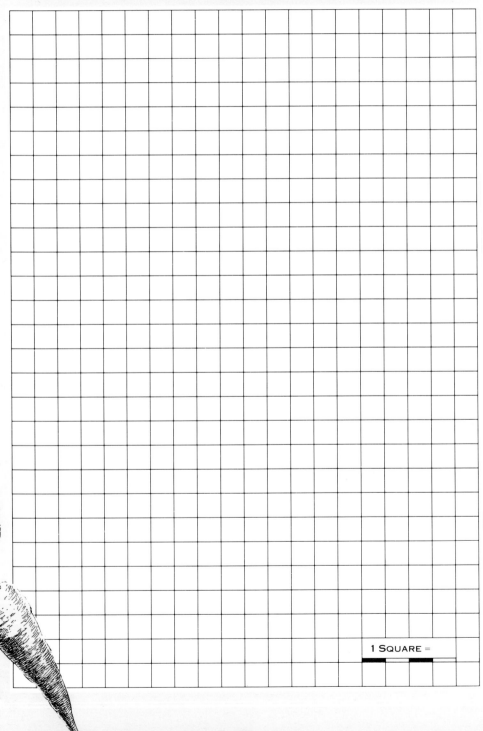

1 SQUARE =

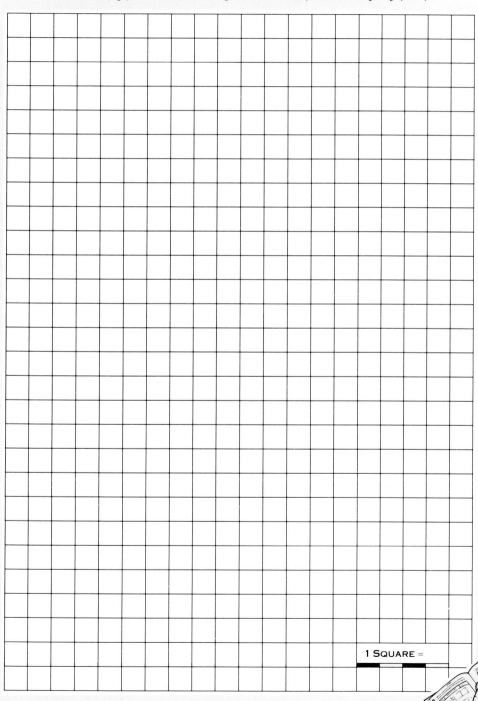

the flow that way. Better by far to pour a few into the palm of your hand and then to
sprinkle them in with your fingers.'
Fred Streeter, quoted in Frank Hennig's *Cheerio Frank, Cheerio Everybody* (1976)

1 SQUARE =

Vegetable Records

VARIETY	SOURCE	DATE SOWN OR PLANTED	LENGTH OF ROW	AMOUNTS OF SEED NO. OF PLANTS

'Records of sowing dates, quantities of seeds or plants needed, cultural details, and pests encountered prove immensely valuable. You may be inundated with advice from experts, but your personal garden diary will be the only source of information about the unique conditions which constitute your garden.'
Joy Larkcom, *Vegetables From Small Gardens* (1976)

DAYS TO GERMINATE	THINNED	PEST/ DISEASE PROBLEMS	CULTURAL NOTES	HARVESTED	REMARKS

Vegetable Records

'I propose . . . to show, that, while, from a very small piece of ground, a large part of the food of a considerable family may be raised, the very act of raising it will be the best possible

VARIETY	SOURCE	DATE SOWN OR PLANTED	LENGTH OF ROW	AMOUNTS OF SEED NO. OF PLANTS
Toms. money Spinner	Rosemary	End April	6 Pots	6
Pears	Packet. Wilkinson	April	8 x 3ft approx	40
R. Beans	Packet, Newsagent	1st week May	1 x 12 ft	20
Potatoes	Newsagent	End April	3ft x 6 plot	40
Blackcurrants	moved	19 Sept-93		4
Redcurrants	moved	''		2
Gooseberries	moved	''		5
Apple Trees	lobbed	18 Sept-93		2
Pear Tree	lobbed	''		1
Greengage	pruned	''		1

NOTES ON GAPS AND GLUTS

foundation of *education* of the children of the labourer; that it will teach them a great number of useful things, *add greatly to their value when they go forth from* their father's home, make them start in life with all possible advantages, and give them the best chance of leading happy lives.'

William Cobbett, *Cottage Economy* (1823)

Days To Germinate	Thinned	Pest/ Disease Problems	Cultural Notes	Harvested	Remarks
		2 pots water logged.			
10	-		Birds eat young plants		
20					
10	-				

Space Savers

With garden space at a premium it's as well to be acquainted with a few space-saving wheezes on the vegetable plot.

Inter-cropping

Between the rows of slow-maturing crops like peas and cabbages, sow fast-maturing crops that will be ready to pick before the main crop needs all the space it's been allowed.

Good inter-crops: radishes, Salad Bowl lettuce, spring onions, turnips.

Catch-cropping

The same quick-maturing crops are used, but here they are sown on ground which is waiting to receive crops like cabbage, cauliflower, brussels sprouts or broccoli later in the season, or which has just yielded an early crop of peas or beans and would otherwise stand idle for the rest of the season.

Cheating

Try growing runner beans up sunflower stems. You'll have to get your sunflowers growing quickly if the beans are to be provided with a decent support!

Grow vegetables in pots on a patio or terrace or as part of a summer bedding scheme. That ubiquitous Salad Bowl lettuce with its frilly green leaves is as bright an edging plant as lobelia and alyssum and you can snip out of it from time to time without ruining the scheme.

Even unused vegetable crops can sometimes have their uses. Leeks that remain uneaten at the end of the season can be planted in a flower border – in their second year they have orbs of bloom that rival any ornamental allium!

The Herb Garden

Herb growing is definitely 'in'. There are those who will tell you they grow a hundred varieties of herbs to use in the kitchen, and there are others who grow just as many but will confess to doing so out of curiosity as much as anything else. I have to admit that I fall into this category myself, relying on mint, basil, thyme, sage and the odd bay leaf to flavour my limited repertoire of gastronomic delights. But I wouldn't be without catnip (which our moggy regularly chews to pieces); or golden-leafed feverfew (which is supposed to be good for migraine but which I grow simply for its brilliant acid-yellow leaves), or costmary, whose leaves make excellent bookmarks!

Mixing herbs in with other border plants is the usual course of action – except for garlic and parsley which are usually consigned to the vegetable plot – but it's far more fun to grow them all together in a proper herb garden, however small it has to be.

Lay an old ladder on the ground and plant up the gap between each rung with a different herb. Or do the same with an old cartwheel (if you just happen to have one lying around). Easier still, make a pattern, any pattern, with some bricks sunk into the earth and plant up the patches of soil between.

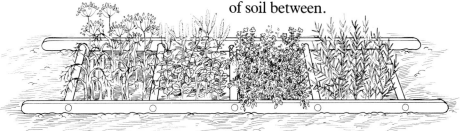

Most herbs love sunshine and don't demand a soil that's rich in manure, so try to give them the conditions they most appreciate. You can mix culinary varieties with decorative herbs like lavender and rue, and a stroll through them on a summer's day will fill your nostrils with scents of the Mediterranean.

A word of warning about mint and lemon balm. They are both thugs. Plant them in sunken, bottomless buckets if you want to prevent them taking over the entire garden.

And finally, somewhere to sit. A garden bench is all very well, but it's not half so aromatic as a chamomile seat. Build a brick 'box' 18 in high, 3 ft long and 18 in wide; fill it with well-rammed soil and plant the top with chamomile spaced 6 in apart. The herb will soon make a dense cushion that's heaven-scent on a warm day.

A Pattern of Herbs

Valuable as they are among other border flowers, herbs seldom look so stunning as when they are grown in their own patch or knot. Seek out the pencil and map your own design opposite, numbering the plants and indicating which is which in the key below.

1	21
2	22
3	23
4	24
5	25
6	26
7	27
8	28
9	29
10	30
11	31
12	32
13	33
14	34
15	35
16	36
17	37
18	38
19	39
20	40

'Herbs are nature's priceless gift to the gardener: the plants are an attractive addition to the flower garden, the fragrant leaves flavour our food and relieve our ailments, and the flowers provide nectar for the bees and petals for pot pourri and other perfumed comforts.'
Rosemary Verey, *The Scented Garden* (1981)

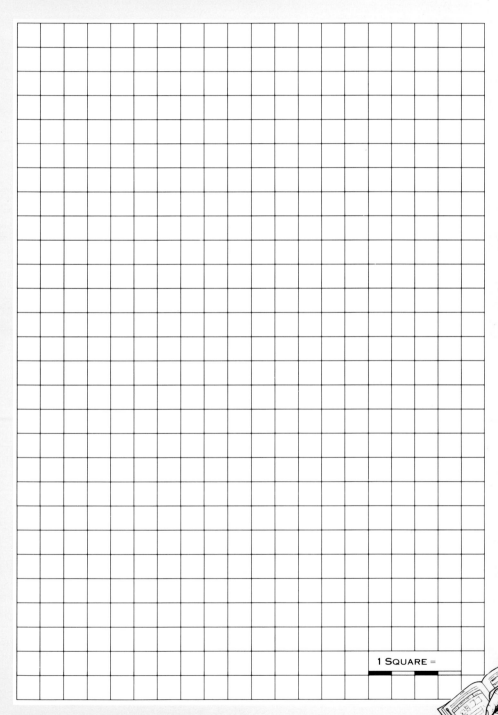

1 SQUARE =

Herb Cropping Records

Variety	Source	Date Sown Or Planted	Site And Soil	Date In Flower

'Jemima Puddleduck was a simpleton: not even the mention of sage and onions made her suspicious.
She went round the farm-garden, nibbling off snippets of all the different sorts of herbs that are used for stuffing roast duck.'
Beatrix Potter, *The Tale of Jemima Puddleduck* (1908)

HEIGHT AND SPREAD	CULTURAL NOTES	HARVESTED	COMMENTS

The Patio

For some reason, any sitting area in the garden that's not made of grass is known nowadays as a patio. The word was originally applied to enclosed courtyards, but there aren't many of those around today, so the usage of the word has been stretched to cover anything remotely flat and solid.

Whatever you call it, it will be one of the most oft-used parts of the garden, so site it with care and consideration. Do you want to sit in sun or shade? If you're a born sun worshipper your patio will be a fat lot of good under a tree. Keep an eye on the path of the sun in relation to parts of your garden and build your patio where the sun stays longest.

I say 'build' deliberately. There's quite a bit of humping and spreading and laying if you do the job properly. But there are short cuts.

The easiest patio to build is one made of washed pea shingle – a sort of smooth gravel sold by builders' merchants. Ram your earth hard and spread a 1½-in layer of shingle on top. Perfectionists will insist on a layer of something called 'scalpings' first, and when rammed hard these do make a better base for the shingle. However, if you're an idler who is prepared to add a bit more shingle should the earth show through, then go ahead without the scalpings.

The beauty of a shingle patio is that foliage and flowering plants can be planted direct into it and shown off to perfection. Any weeds that come through can be bumped off with a can of contact weedkiller, but you'd be well advised to clear any thick-rooted weeds from the ground before you start.

There are a couple of disadvantages to gravel: your chairlegs will sometimes refuse to stop wobbling, and children find the surface difficult to ride bikes on. Mind you, that could be a distinct advantage.

Flagstones, bricks, slabs and crazy paving are more usually chosen as patio bases. Lay them on a *dry* mix of five parts sand to one part cement, and point them with the same *dry* mixture. The stuff will draw moisture from the soil below to set it and you'll not be left with nasty cement stains on your stonework which is what happens if you use wet cement.

Of course there's always the more up-market timber decking, but it does tend to be slippery in wet weather and it doesn't last as long as stone.

How about size? Make the area as large as you can – it's amazing just how much room a table and four chairs or a couple of sunloungers take up. And you still want to be able to weave your way between them with a tray of drinks.

If you get a few good summers, your patio will, with any luck, turn into an outdoor room, so allow for features such as a barbecue – actually building them into the scheme for preference. (A brick-built barbecue is far cheaper and far longer-lasting than one of those pricy tin kettle-drums on wheels.)

The greatest charm of your outdoor room lies in the planting. Don't stint yourself; do it well. Large flowerpots (at least 10 in diameter), tubs, urns and troughs will all support a wide range of plants. Even trees can be grown in tubs; they'll have to be found another home when they outgrow their welcome, but for the most part a bit of stature will be welcomed. You can grow *anything* in a pot for a few years at least, and by moving the containers around you can change the scene – every day if you're feeling strong.

One thing you must remember about plants in pots and tubs is that they depend on you for water and food. Small pots dry out two or three times a day in summer, which is why it makes sense to choose larger ones, but you'll still have to make the daily round with the can or hose. It's a small price to pay for such a restful delight.

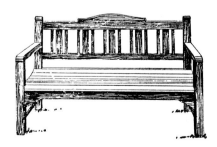

Patio Plan

The reclining chair and the drinks table will take up far more room than you'd think. Plan your patio well, both in shape and scale, and allow for wads of colour and fragrance that can be appreciated without raising more than your head from the cushions of the chair.

Symbols

Tree   Deciduous shrub

Evergreen shrub   Border plants

Containers

'A patio is as much a dream garden as Chatsworth or Sissinghurst and gives far less trouble.'
Anne Scott-James, *The Pleasure Garden* (1977)

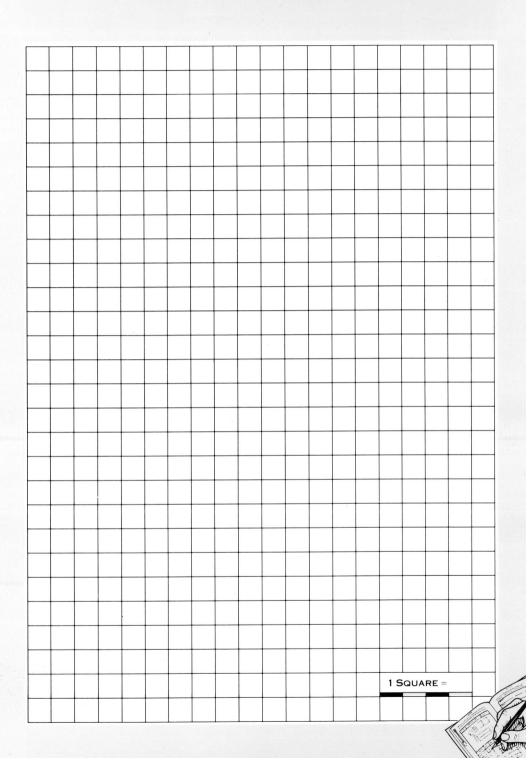

1 SQUARE =

The Fruit Garden

You'll have to be a fairly keen gardener to run a vegetable plot, but even the reluctant grower can manage the odd fruit bush without too much hassle. If I were allowed to grow only one fruit it would be the raspberry. It can be squeezed in alongside a fence in gardens where space is short, and there are some varieties that fruit in summer and others that produce a later crop in autumn. Try Zeva as an autumn fruiter; it's a real cracker.

For other folk, strawberries remain the firm favourite, and again they can be picked right through the summer according to variety, and fitted into an even smaller plot, balcony or window-box than raspberries. Choose strawberries carefully: always try a few fruits of any variety before you commit yourself to a plantation. Some modern strawberries are healthy growers with fat, red berries, but they lack that sweetness possessed by good old favourites like Royal Sovereign. Don't bother with this last-named variety nowadays; it's far too prone to virus diseases. If you're looking for a good substitute, try Tenira.

No English garden of any size is complete without its regulation apple tree. Don't panic; it doesn't have to grow twenty feet tall and as much across. Today you can buy trees grafted on to dwarfing rootstocks that will keep them well within reach at fruit picking time, and they'll even start to crop earlier in their life. Rootstocks have mysterious-sounding numbers. If you want a dwarfing one, simply remember the numbers: M9 and M27. Any nurseryman worth his salt will know what you're rambling on about and should do his best to supply the right thing.

As to variety, again it's a matter of taste. But do remember that Cox's Orange Pippin is really an orchard apple. It needs regular spraying to do well. You'll do far better selecting a variety like Spartan if you're planning to have a single tree that won't be sprayed much. All fruit trees carry better crops if there are others in the near vicinity to assist with cross-pollination. If no-one near you has an apple or pear to mate with yours, then you'd better buy two or three, and check again with your nurseryman that the varieties you buy are suitable pollinators for one another. It's getting a bit complicated isn't it?

Never mind; plums like Victoria and damsons like Merryweather can usually set a fair crop on their own. However, they do make rather larger trees than dwarf apples, and if any plant of stature is simply too big to contemplate then settle for soft fruits like gooseberries and currants.

Of all fruit bushes, gooseberries must be the most obliging. With no fuss at all they'll produce for you a fat and tasty harvest of green, yellow or dark red fruits that can be jammed, pied or fooled. Currants are, I suppose, more of an acquired taste in the red and white varieties, but blackcurrants will perk up your plain old apple pies and fill up your shelves with jams and jellies full of dark, rich promise.

It really is as easy as that, provided no nasty little pest or disease decides to wreak havoc in your orchard. Don't despair; it doesn't happen too often, and if you spread your fruits around the garden at least the pests will have to look harder to find them!

Fruit Records

Few gardens contain fruits grouped together in one spot, so it's hardly necessary to plan a fruit plot. Instead, keep notes of the performance of your plants, their cropping ability and whether or not you like what they give. A note of those all-too-necessary sprays to banish maggots and bugs will also be of great value (in assessing whether or not they work, as much as anything else!).

VARIETY	SOURCE	PLANTING DATE	SITE AND SOIL	PRUNED	HARVESTED
B. Currant	Empire	Nov 89			
Gooseberry	Empire	Nov 89			
R. Currant	Empire	Nov 89			
Strawberrys	Empire	Nov 89			
Rhubarb	Cold Store	Summer 89			
Plum	Here				
Apple	Here				
Greengage	Here				
Pear	Here				
Raspberry	Helen	Sept 89			

'. . . granting the English prepossession for a firm-fleshed apple with a touch of briskness and tang behind its sweetness and spiciness, the superiority of the English apples *here* is outside disputation.'
Sir A. Daniel Hall, *The Apple* (1933)

PESTS AND DISEASES	SPRAYED	OTHER TREATMENT	REMARKS

Hedges, Fences, Walls and Windbreaks

I've never believed that a garden is a place for socializing with the neighbours. It's alright if they're invited, but I'd far rather nip out there unobserved on most occasions and that's why I value my hedges.

If you plan to plant one, do remember a few things: a hedge lasts for a long while, so give it plenty of manure when you plant; allow room to clip it (probably twice a year); remember that its roots will invade any adjacent border; remember that it will cast shade on all but northern boundaries. And if at all possible, don't plant privet – we've enough of that already. There's a host of hedging plants that carry flowers and fruits and which have decorative leaves; they are far better to look at than privet. And yes, I know that Leyland cypress is tempting because it grows fast. It makes a good, thick hedge, too. But if your garden is small it will swamp you unless you clip it regularly. Think carefully.

Fences are an easier bet in that they don't need clipping, but they are costlier to put up in the first place and they can look incredibly dull unless covered with foliage. Use them as supports for climbing roses, clematises, climbing nasturtiums and other creepers, mixing flowering and foliage climbers together for year-round effect. Not all of them will cling unaided, so provide the scrambling types with a few horizontal wires to give them a leg up.

Make house walls a part of your garden, too. Wired in the same way as garden fences (with strands of plastic-coated wire fixed at 18-in intervals up the face of the brickwork) they can be cheered up with a vast range of climbers and wall shrubs. None of these will do any harm to your foundations, but they'll really appreciate plenty of organic enrichment at planting time and copious supplies of water during their first year of establishment. Try planting ivies and clematises alongside one another, or the Chilean glory flower (eccremocarpus) next to a firethorn (pyracantha) so that it clambers through the evergreen leaves and decorates them with its summer flowers.

In exposed gardens that are swept by wind you'll have to do something to interrupt its flow if your plants are to settle in rather than dry out. Tough hedges like hawthorn will do the job, or you can resort to wattle hurdles for instant protection.

Individual shrubs can be protected for a month or two if they are surrounded by a sacking screen, or an old plastic fertilizer sack slit top and bottom to make a tube. Push in three or four canes around the plant to be protected, and drop the tube over the top. It looks horrible but it does the trick!

Water Gardening

The chances are that you'll get more pleasure from a garden pool than any other single feature on your plot; or at least your children will. Aside from the water lily, the bog irises and the monkey flowers that grow in and around it there's an amazing amount of wildlife to be observed. Frogs and toads will come to stay (don't spurn them, they're excellent slug catchers); dragonflies and damsel flies will zip over the water in summer, along with pond skaters and water boatmen, and you can brighten up the murky depths with fish. It's irresistible!

All you have to do is find the right spot. Don't make your pond under a tree; it will be shaded (which the plants won't like) and every autumn you'll have to net it to prevent leaves from filling it to the brim. No; plonk it in the open. As far as size and shape go, make your pond as large as possible and keep the shape simple. A depth of 18 in is ample, with a shelf where the water is about 10 in deep running right round the inside. This is for the plants that don't like their water really deep; 'marginal aquatics', they're called.

Don't think that your pond must be lined with concrete – those days are gone. Instead look for a butyl liner or (second choice) one made from PVC. If funds are really short you can always use thick polythene, but you'll have to replace it every two or three years. Butyl lasts much, much longer.

When your hole is dug, knock down any protruding stones with the back of the spade and then line the hole with sheets of newspaper. Lower the liner into place, checking that it is evenly distributed, and then start to fill it with water. As soon as the final water level is reached, stop filling and start masking your edge.

Paving stones are really the most effective edgers. Position them so that they overhang the water by a couple of inches and completely hide the liner from view. Once they're all in position the construction work is finished. Now you can think about planting.

Don't overdo it. The water's surface is as valuable for its reflective properties as it is for supporting plants, so don't cover it all up. First put in some oxygenating plants to keep the water in good order and to help prevent it turning green. New ponds always turn green a few days after being filled, so don't go and empty yours as soon as it shows a sign of pea soup. Be patient, and if you've dropped in plenty of those little clumps of elodea it should eventually sort itself out.

The water lily and the marginal aquatics, all planted in plastic baskets of ordinary garden soil, can go in next, but then wait for a couple of weeks before introducing any fish. Allow a couple of square feet of pool surface area for each fish, and stick to golden orfe and plain goldfish unless you're confident that those expensive koi carp will survive.

You'll have problems from time to time. Green blanket weed will proliferate in certain weathers but is easy enough to fish out with a wire-toothed rake; and any dead water lily leaves are best cut off before they foul the water.

But these ministrations are small price to pay for the pleasure the pond provides at every other season. And if all this seems like an arduous slog, get yourself half a beer barrel, fill it with water, plonk a pygmy water lily in it, along with two goldfish for company, and there you are; an instant patio pool.

THE GARDENER'S LOGBOOK

Pool Plan

'The common frog, for example, is no longer common in many areas as a result of filling in of country ponds and the widespread use of pesticides which seep into the remaining ponds and kill off many of their inhabitants. A network of garden ponds will do much to ensure the

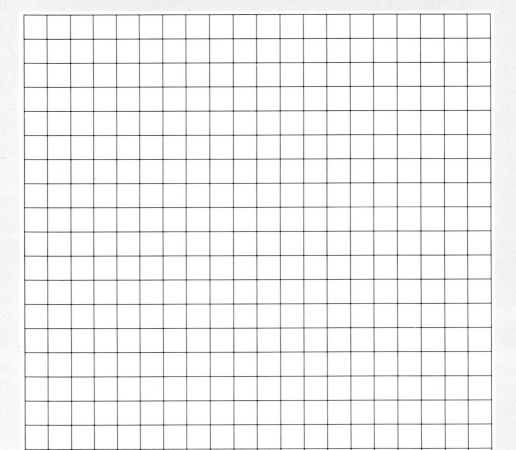

1 SQUARE =

survival of this fascinating and useful creature and to ensure that future generations of little boys will be able to indulge in the wonderful pastime of catching wriggly tadpoles or pollywogs and keeping them (temporarily, I hope) in a jam jar.'
Michael Chinery, *The Natural History of the Garden* (1977)

LIVESTOCK	SOURCE	REMARKS

PLANT	SOURCE	DATE PLANTED	REMARKS

Utility Areas

No-one would claim that the compost heap was the most eye-catching feature in their garden, but all too often its unglamorous image results in it being stuck under a tree in a distant corner where it gradually spreads into an eyesore that rivals the corporation rubbish tip. Put it under the tree if you must, but make for it a restraining container that ensures you can scoop up some rotted matter for soil enrichment when the bacteria have done their work.

Two heaps are better than one – one to be filling and the other one full and rotting. Make them 4 ft square and 4 ft high, with wire netting or timber sides fastened to stout posts. One side should be removable so that you can get the rotten stuff out at the bottom.

Build up your heap by mixing the ingredients as you apply them: annual weeds, vegetable waste, tea leaves, grass clippings and crushed egg shells. Don't put on the heap thick-rooted perennial weeds, woody stems or household food.

After every 9 in layer, sprinkle on a couple of handfuls of sulphate of ammonia or compost accelerator plus a few handfuls of garden soil. Keep the top of the heap covered with a bit of old carpet or sacking and water it in dry weather.

You'll be able to dig lovely, crumbly brown stuff out of the bottom between three and six months after putting it there. Free enrichment!

And what of the uncompostables? Some can go in the dustbin, but sticks and woody stuff you may feel have to be burned. Keep a space for this job, too. And a metal incinerator. If you dry the rubbish first it will make far less smoke when you burn it, and provided you don't do the job on a sunny day you shouldn't offend the neighbours.

There is one luxury item in the utilitarian garden: a potting shed. I've just built one. It's a fabulous haven among composts and fertilizers and flowerpots and forks. As an escape from the family I recommend it with no reservations at all!

Foods and Fertilizers

Are you baffled by bonemeal; foxed by fish manure and puzzled by potash? There's no need to be. If you're looking for a few useful fertilizers and manures for your garden, these are the ones I'd recommend:

Blood, bone and fishmeal
A good, all-round fertilizer for anything that grows. I apply it at the rate of two clenched fistfuls to the square yard at any time from March to September.

Rose fertilizer
Superb for flowering shrubs and border plants of any kind. Contains lots of potash which promotes flowering and fruiting. Use between April and August; one fistful per square yard.

Sulphate of ammonia
Full of nitrogen which promotes green, leafy growth. Very strong. Use at the rate of half a clenched fistful to the square yard on the lawn and the compost heap. Water the lawn after a day if no rain falls or it may scorch the grass. Good for giving garden plants a boost if they're reluctant to grow.

Tomato fertilizer
Good for tomatoes and anything else that flowers or fruits. Use a liquid variety as per instructions on label.

Optional extras

Growmore
As for blood, bone and fish, but not so good.

Bonemeal
Often recommended for use at planting time, but overrated.

Sulphate of potash
Use as an alternative to rose or tomato fertilizer.

When it comes to heavy manures, here's what to do with them:

Peat
Contains no nourishment, so valuable only as a soil conditioner. Dig it in; or use it around the roots at planting time.

Animal manure
Good soil enrichment. Dig in in autumn or use as a surface mulch in spring, but watch out for any germinating weed seeds it may contain.

Leafmould
Dig in during autumn, or use as a surface mulch in spring. Not many nutrients.

Shredded bark
Best, long-lasting mulch. Use in spring. Scatter fertilizer first. Don't dig in, for it robs soil of nitrogen while it's breaking down.

House Plants

Even the most reluctant gardener has house plants, and probably treats them like pieces of furniture. That would explain why they die in their thousands.

But provided you choose the right plant for your particular circumstances it will thrive with comparatively little attention. Nevertheless, you must be prepared to give it just a fraction more care than you lavish on your armchair.

Light

All plants need light to grow, but some need more light than others. Hold a newspaper at arm's length in a shady corner of your room. Can you still read it? If you can, then the aspidistra, the grape ivy, and one or two other shade tolerators will probably survive there. If you can't read the print, there are two assumptions to be made. Either (a) it is too dark a spot for any house plant to survive, or (b) you need spectacles.

Flowering plants, as a rule, need the most light. Site them near a window but take care to ensure that they are never scorched by bright sunlight. Most plants are happiest about three or four feet from a window where they will receive good indirect light.

Temperature

There's no point in adjusting your lifestyle to suit your house plants, so buy those that can fit in with your existing way of life. Most house plants enjoy the warmth of central heating; some others prefer it cooler – ivies and cyclamen, for instance.

Humidity

Few plants relish really dry air, so if your central heating is fierce, stand your house plants on trays of gravel that is kept constantly moist. It's the only way to keep ferns alive in most households, and it's so much easier than spraying the plants once a day with tepid water – this effect doesn't last very long and it plays havoc with your french-polished Chippendale chiffonier.

Water

It's the staff of life to all plants, but most house plants are killed by it. Too much of it drives all air from the compost and the plants quite literally drown. As a rule of thumb, all house plants should be watered only when the surface of the compost in the pot feels dry. Then they should be left alone until the compost dries once more. Only ferns, Christmas azaleas, cyperus (umbrella grass) and bromeliads (relatives of the pineapple) relish being kept moist at all times.

All plants need more water in summer than they do in winter.

Keep your finger on the compost and you won't go far wrong.

Food

Feed your house plants once a fortnight between April and September. Only winter-flowering plants need to be fed between October and March; the rest are happy to slow down. Use a general liquid feed for foliage plants, and tomato fertilizer for flowering pot plants – it works wonders.

Repotting

Most house plants are ready for a larger pot of fresh compost every other year. Give them a container two inches larger in diameter and use either a peat-based compost, or John Innes No 2 potting compost. The latter is heavier and useful where tall plants are being grown (it prevents them from falling over).

Spring is the best time to repot all plants, and they won't need feeding for at least six weeks afterwards.

Pinching and staking

Never be frightened of pinching out the shoot tips of plants to make them bushy (unless their charm lies in the single-stemmed look). Tall plants should be staked if they look like toppling, but try to do the job so that the support looks as unobtrusive as possible. Moss-covered stakes are quite useless; all they do is shower your carpet with the dry moss that's impossible to keep moist in the average sitting room. Use them only in greenhouses where water can be regularly splashed about.

Pests and diseases

Act quickly when you spot trouble. It usually manifests itself in the form of sticky leaves that are covered with a sooty mould. This is a fungus that grows on the honeydew secreted either by greenfly, whitefly, mealy bugs or scale insects, any of which and all of which can attack house plants.

Spray with a systemic insecticide at the first sign of trouble, but take the plant outdoors first and bring it back in once the foliage is dry. Repeat sprays will be necessary every ten days until you are sure that no more youngsters are emerging.

Regular leaf cleaning with rainwater to which a little milk has been added will keep the leaves sparkling clean and less prone to attack by diseases.

House Plant Records

You can best cater for the quirks of your house plants if you keep a note of what you've done to them and when. That way they are far less likely to starve to death or die of neglect. Mind you, you'll still have to make sure you don't fuss them to death. More house plants die of drowning than anything else!

PLANT	DATE ACQUIRED	POSITION	APPROX. TEMP.	FEEDING NOTES

'The majority of problems with houseplants can be avoided by a little common sense and remembering, in the words of the old saying, that prevention is better than cure . . . Each plant is an individual, with its own characteristics and quirks.'
William Davidson, *The Houseplant Survival Manual* (1982)

EPOTTED	SPRAYED	IN FLOWER	OTHER TREATMENT	PERFORMANCE

House Plant Records

PLANT	DATE ACQUIRED	POSITION	APPROX. TEMP.	FEEDING NOTES

'We must also remember that plants in pots must have a lot of attention. We cannot treat them as mere ornaments which only need dusting. They require watering, cleaning, occasional feeding and repotting. Anyone who is not prepared to give his plants at least an hour's attention every week will inevitably fail with them.'
Anthony Huxley, *House Plants, Cacti and Succulents* (1972)

REPOTTED	SPRAYED	IN FLOWER	OTHER TREATMENT	PERFORMANCE

Pests and Diseases

The mention of chemicals has an amazing effect on the blood pressure of some gardeners. Suggest to them that they should spray the greenfly on their roses and they'll take great offence and accuse you of polluting the atmosphere and destroying the balance of nature.

They have a point. The wanton splashing around of an assortment of chemicals by folk who don't know what they're doing is a terrifying prospect. But is it so irresponsible to select a chemical that's been developed after years of research and shown to control the pest or disease in question and yet leave other forms of life unharmed? I think not.

True enough, not all chemicals are selective in their action, but some are now appearing which are, and it is these, in moderation, that I like to recommend.

Pretending that pests and diseases will go away if you turn your back is just plain nonsense. Greenfly may look innocent, but their crime is not simply one of cluttering up the plant by being there. They suck its sap, weaken it, secrete sticky honeydew which is gathered by ants and which the black sooty mould grows upon, and they transmit virus diseases which stunt and deform plant leaves and stems. Can you really afford to leave them alone?

One acquaintance suggested that the best cure for greenfly on my plum tree was to spray it with soapy water. I did so and the greenfly died. But so did the leaves – the mixture scorched them and turned them brown.

Now I use a chemical that's called a specific aphicide. It kills greenfly, blackfly and all related shades but not bees, ladybirds and lacewings, all of which are beneficial. The chemical is called pirimicarb, and it's sold as ICI Rapid Greenfly Killer.

You must decide for yourself just how much spraying you want to do. There are winter washes to kill overwintering eggs and insects on fruit trees; fungicides to kill fungi; insecticides to kill insects and acaricides to kill menacing mites like red spider.

I don't winter wash my trees. I cope with a few maggoty apples and lichens on the branches. I do, however, give an occasional blast of a 'cocktail mixture' to my roses to control insect pests as well as mildew and blackspot which I know are going to strike every year unless I do something about it. Prevention is better than cure, they say, but I only bother trying to prevent things which I know are going to attack. And that includes slugs.

I use those tiny 'mini-pellets' that are coloured bright blue. I scatter them very thinly among susceptible border plants like hostas, and once these beauties are more than four inches above the soil they manage to fend for themselves. I've heard stories about family pets being poisoned by slug pellets, but so far as I know this has only happened when the animals have got at the packet. As to the cry that poisoned slugs will poison the hedgehogs and thrushes that eat them I can only inquire where the proof is for such accusations.

If you refuse to use poisoned pellets then you must resort to that amusing method of slug control, the beer trap. Sink empty cream or yoghurt pots into the ground among susceptible plants, fill them with beer and wait for the slugs to dive in – they do so in their hundreds. What a way to go!

But if all this warfare is beginning to sound too sinister, remember that you can do a lot to prevent attack by pests and diseases simply by being a good gardener. Ensure that your plants are never short of water or food – plants that are well cared for are less likely to be devastated by a pest or disease.

Buy healthy plants in the first place, from a grower who runs a clean nursery. Be clean and tidy yourself – many diseases overwinter on weeds, and pests lurk unseen in piles of rubbish.

Snip out dead wood and remove faded leaves and flowers to prevent the rot setting in. Use chemicals with care. And keep your fingers crossed.

Pests and Diseases

There's often no cause to blame yourself when pests and diseases strike, but you will probably kick yourself if you forget the name of the product or treatment that did well for you last year, or which was a signal failure. Make notes of the problems, the attempted remedies and the results; it could double your efficiency next year !

PROBLEM	PLANTS ATTACKED	TREATMENT	DATE	EFFECTIVE?

'Gardening, like love, is a funny thing; and doesn't always yield to analysis.'
H.E. Bates, *A Love of Flowers* (1971)

PROBLEM	PLANTS ATTACKED	TREATMENT	DATE	EFFECTIVE?

A Gardener's Calendar

As if you hadn't enough to worry about, here are a few memory-joggers to take you through the year.

JANUARY

Prune roses. Order seeds from catalogues. Plant bare-root trees and shrubs. Prune fruit trees and bushes. Winter wash fruit trees. Dig the vegetable plot. Firm in plants lifted by frost. Prune outdoor vines. Place cloches over ground to be sown with early vegetable crops. Scrub down empty greenhouses. Prune wisteria. Feed garden birds. Prepare runner bean trenches. Lay turf in mild spells. Send mowers for servicing. Clean and repair garden tools.

FEBRUARY

Clip over heathers as their flowers fade. Plant lily bulbs. Prune roses. Prune summer-flowering shrubs. Continue to plant trees and shrubs. Plant herbaceous perennials. Spray peaches to control leaf curl. Prune raspberries. Plant shallots. Sow early vegetables under cloches. Plant Jerusalem artichokes. Force outdoor rhubarb. Sow bedding plants in a heated greenhouse, and start dahlia tubers into growth. Pollinate greenhouse-grown peaches, apricots and nectarines. Prune winter-flowering shrubs as their blooms fade. Feed fruit trees and bushes. Pot up rooted house plant and greenhouse plant cuttings. Take chrysanthemum and carnation cuttings. Spike lawns. Water camellias, rhododendrons and azaleas with iron sequestrene. Complete fruit tree pruning. Plant rhubarb. Rest cyclamen after flowering. Lay turf.

MARCH

Lift and divide overcrowded snowdrops. Prune figs. Complete rose pruning. Plant strawberries. Sow vegetables. Repot house plants. Prick out seedlings. Lift and divide large clumps of border plants. Lay turf. Sow hardy annuals outdoors. Complete fruit tree planting. Spray outdoor peaches to control leaf curl. Control slugs. Plant early potatoes. Take cuttings of pelargoniums and other pot plants. Spike and scarify lawns. Scatter fertilizer among border plants and hoe it in. Mulch raspberries and fruit bushes. Sow herbs in a cold frame. Sow more bedding plants. Plant gladioli. Plant onion sets. Sow sweet peas outdoors. Mulch beds and borders.

APRIL

Start to mow lawns. Plant out faded pot-grown bulbs. Complete planting of border perennials. Sow more hardy annuals. Continue to plant gladioli. Construct rock gardens and plant alpines. Plant evergreens. Prune

established evergreens. Hoe to keep down weeds. Sow more vegetables.
Plant maincrop potatoes. Plant globe artichokes. Sow tomatoes,
cucumbers and melons. Prick out seedlings. Take cuttings from
sprouting dahlia tubers. Repot house plants. Prune forsythia. Sow new
lawns. Take cuttings of border plants. Sow more vegetables. Plant
asparagus. Prune buddleias. Plant out sweet peas sown under glass.
Construct garden pools. Prune young plum trees. Spray with care to
control greenfly. Thin vegetable seedlings. Plant begonia and gloxinia
corms. Feed rose bushes. Remove faded flowerheads from daffodils.

MAY
Stake border plants. Harden off bedding plants. Apply fertilizer and
weedkiller dressing to lawns. Continue to sow new lawns and patch old
ones. Plant up garden pools. Mow lawns weekly. Lay straw among
strawberries to protect fruits. Erect runner bean supports. Hoe regularly
to keep down weeds. Sow more vegetables and hardy annuals. Plant up
hanging baskets and window-boxes. Spray roses to control greenfly,
mildew and blackspot. Plant winter cabbages, cauliflowers and sprouts.
Earth up potatoes. Sow runner beans. Stake gladioli. Plant out early-
flowering chrysanthemums. Plant dahlia tubers. Harvest asparagus. Plant
tomatoes in unheated greenhouses. Start to feed pot plants once a
fortnight. Lift and divide polyanthuses. Stake hardy annuals. Remove
strawberry runners. Protect strawberries from birds. Shade greenhouses.
Plant out bedding late in the month in southern counties.

JUNE
Plant out bedding early in the month. Clip evergreen hedges. Hang up
hanging baskets. Mow lawns regularly. Water plants with a sprinkler in
spells of drought. Plant cucumbers and melons in unheated greenhouses.
Sow and plant more vegetables. Sow wallflowers and sweet williams
outdoors for next spring's bedding. Tie in blackberry and loganberry
shoots. Thin overcrowded fruits on apples, pears and peaches. Summer
prune gooseberries and currants. Stop harvesting asparagus. Earth
up potatoes and leeks. Pot up rooted cuttings. Feed tomatoes
weekly. Train cucumbers and melons. Stand pot plants outdoors
for summer. Lift and divide overcrowded clumps of large-flowered
irises. Take pot plant cuttings. Lift and dry off tulip and hyacinth
bulbs. Remove rose suckers. Thin vegetable seedlings.

JULY
Shorten long growths on wisteria. Take cuttings from shrubs.
Remove faded flowers from shrubs and border plants. Mow

A Gardener's Calendar

lawns regularly. Irrigate in dry spells. Water hanging baskets and other containers daily. Summer-prune trained and pot-grown apple trees. Pollinate melons. Pinch male flowers from cucumbers. Mulch runner beans. Hoe to keep down weeds. Sow more vegetables. Pot up rooted cuttings. Remove sideshoots from tomatoes. Transplant wallflowers and other spring bedding plants. Plant container-grown shrubs. Cut and dry herbs for winter use. Take pot plant cuttings. Fumigate greenhouses to control pests. Feed greenhouse plants once a week.

AUGUST
Stake dahlias. Plant madonna lilies. Mow lawns regularly. Water all container-grown plants and hanging baskets daily if necessary. Clip hedges. Dead-head flowering plants. Irrigate when necessary. Continue to plant container-grown shrubs except in severe drought. Cut out raspberry canes when their crop has been picked. Plant new strawberry beds. Allow onions to ripen in the sun. Sow more vegetables. Take cuttings of shrubs and pot plants. Plant autumn-flowering crocuses and colchicums, and hardy cyclamen. Pick early apples. Pot up freesia corms for winter flowers. Pot up rooted cuttings. Prune rambling roses that have finished flowering. Disbud dahlias. Cut and dry everlasting flowers. Sow cyclamen. Sow winter lettuces in greenhouse borders.

SEPTEMBER
Sow new lawns. Take cuttings of roses and root them outdoors. Plant winter-flowering bulbs in pots and spring-flowering bulbs outdoors. Lay turf. Take cuttings of evergreens and conifers. Sow hardy annuals outdoors for flowers next summer. Mow lawns. Dead-head roses and border plants. Harvest apples and pears. Plant strawberries. Take cuttings of gooseberries and root outdoors. Plant spring cabbages. Store onions. Sow more vegetables. Clear out cucumbers and melons that have finished cropping. Take pelargonium cuttings. Pot up rooted cuttings. Plant lily bulbs. Pull up faded hardy annuals. Order trees and shrubs and fruit for autumn planting. Store root vegetables. Pot up lily bulbs. Store apples and pears. Pot up hippeastrum bulbs. Lift and store potatoes. Bring pot plants indoors if they have been stood outside for summer. Remove greenhouse shading.

OCTOBER
Clear beds and borders of summer bedding. Dig up and store gladioli. Plant wallflowers and other spring bedding plants. Lay turf. Spike and scarify lawns. Plant conifers and other evergreens. Continue to plant

spring-flowering bulbs. Plant lilies. Pick and store fruits. Prune blackberries and loganberries. Lift and store potatoes and root vegetables. Plant spring cabbages. Pot up mint roots for windowsill supplies in winter. Take hardwood cuttings of shrubs and root outdoors. Plant border plants and container-grown shrubs. Lift and store dahlia tubers once foliage is blackened. Prepare ground for autumn planting of trees, border plants, shrubs and fruit. Cut down asparagus and globe artichokes. Start to dig vegetable plot. Keep greenhouse plants free of faded leaves and flowers.

NOVEMBER

Give the lawn a final cut. Protect tender plants with straw or bracken. Complete planting of spring-flowering bulbs. Lay turf. Cut down border perennials. Plant new border perennials. Plant bare-root trees, shrubs and fruits. Sweep up and stack fallen leaves. Check fruits in store and remove those that are rotting. Sow hardy broad beans. Continue to dig vegetable plot. Bring in bulbs potted in early September. Clip deciduous hedges. Prune fruit trees.

DECEMBER

Continue to dig bare ground. Prune roses. Bring bulbs in pots indoors. Force rhubarb in a greenhouse. Force chicory. Protect developing cauliflower curds. Cloche Christmas roses. Prune *Clematis* x *jackmanii* hard back. Lay paving and erect and repair fences. Lag outside water taps. Continue to sweep and stack leaves. Lay turf in fine weather. Keep pot plants on the dry side in cool rooms and greenhouses. Erect a new compost bin if necessary. Spike waterlogged lawns. Spray fruit trees with winter wash.Clean the greenhouse. Continue to plant trees, shrubs and fruits. Plant border perennials when the ground is in good condition. Send off for seed catalogues. Check that tree ties are secure but not too tight.

Winter Planning

We are lucky in Britain (though you might not think so on a windy, rain-lashed November day) to have a spell of enforced rest while nature, with a freezing hand, sweeps up and sterilizes the garden. Use the time to muse over your successes and failures, and jot them down, lest you forget. Plants to order. Plants to ditch. Plants to move, and plants to give away to those who've been wise enough to admire them.

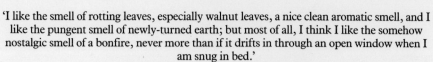

'I like the smell of rotting leaves, especially walnut leaves, a nice clean aromatic smell, and I like the pungent smell of newly-turned earth; but most of all, I think I like the somehow nostalgic smell of a bonfire, never more than if it drifts in through an open window when I am snug in bed.'
Valerie Finnis, *A Gardener's Dozen* (1980)

The Gardener's Library

I write these words in a room lined with gardening books. I'm an addict. I've only to set eyes on a second-hand bookshop to be filled with an inquisitive desire to comb its shelves for curiosities and bargains that I can take home and gloat over and usually read.

Serious book collectors will acquire anything that has value, but I've always restrained myself from buying any book I couldn't actually use either as a source of inspiration in my gardening or as a source of information for writing. This has two effects: the first is that it prevents my shelves from being filled up at a rate of knots, and the second is that it prevents me from getting frowned on by my wife who reads the bank statements.

Take to garden book collecting and you can quickly spend a fortune, especially on finely coloured tomes of the nineteenth century. No; I'd rather relinquish the responsibility of owning such works of art and stick to more practical volumes.

These fall, basically, into two categories: reference works that are to be delved into and plundered whenever a question about the growing technique or country of origin of a plant is in doubt; and those which provide their information in an entertaining and readable way.

It's the latter that I find irresistible, and they are not always old. If you're looking for 'a good read', keep your eye open for books written by Christopher Lloyd, Beth Chatto and Anne Scott-James. Graham Stuart Thomas is another writer with a large fan club – he's the topmost authority on old shrub roses and quite hot on border plants, too. For general information you'll have to go a long way to beat Arthur Hellyer.

The great garden writers of yesteryear have turned into legends. Grab anything written by E.A. Bowles, Vita Sackville-West, A.T. Johnson and William Robinson. Gertrude Jekyll was a pioneer of garden planning and colour scheming, and Mrs C.W. Earle offers a fascinating 'period read' on gardening for well-to-do ladies.

As to fashionable volumes, there are many. Aficionados will know and love Russell Page's *The Education of a Gardener*; alpine enthusiasts dip into and drool over Reginald Farrer's *The English Rock Garden*, and tree and shrub fans will forever cherish their four-volume collection of W.J. Bean's *Trees and Shrubs Hardy in the British Isles*. Save up for it; a current set will cost you £160. Cheaper and equally essential is *Hiller's Manual of Trees and Shrubs*; concise, valuable stuff here.

Hundreds of new gardening books are published every year, and you'll have to sift through them to sort the wheat from the chaff. Every

year produces its smattering of future standard works – the trick is to spot them and invest quickly.

If you'd rather shop for second-hand books, then write to one of the firms listed below for their catalogue. But be warned; once you're hooked on this book collecting lark it will cost you dearly in terms of shelving!

Daniel Lloyd, Heather Lea, Hillcrest Avenue, Chertsey, Surrey.
Mike Park, 119 South Park Road, Wimbledon, London SW19.

The Gardener's Library

There's only one thing nearly as good as gardening, and that's reading about it. Record the books from your shelf that give particular pleasure, and those that offer elusive information that you're likely to need again.

AUTHOR & TITLE	REMARKS

'And what is the use of a book,' thought Alice, 'without pictures or conversation?'
Lewis Carroll, *Alice's Adventures in Wonderland* (1865)

AUTHOR & TITLE	REMARKS

The Gardener's Directory

Names and addresses are elusive, so here are some that you might find useful during the course of your gardening year. I've listed the most important organizations, and some nurseries that offer unusual or uncommon plants that don't turn up at every garden centre. The names of rose nurseries and suppliers of common bulbs are easy enough to find in all sorts of magazines; those included in my little bunch are smaller, but all the more fascinating for that.

I don't offer any kind of guarantee with this list, but I will say that the nurseries mentioned are well established and have been used by keen gardeners for a good number of years.

Organizations and Societies

Royal Horticultural Society, Vincent Square, London SW1.

Royal National Rose Society, Bone Hill, St Albans, Herts.

Alpine Garden Society, Lye End Link, St Johns, Woking, Surrey.

Hardy Plant Society, 10 St Barnabas Road, Emmer Green, Caversham, Reading, Berks.

Arboricultural Association, Ampfield House, Ampfield, Romsey, Hants.

Henry Doubleday Research Association, Convent Lane, Bocking, Braintree, Essex. *(Organic gardening)*

Herb Society, 34 Boscobel Place, London SW1.

National Association of Flower Arrangement Societies of Great Britain, 21a Denbigh Street, London SW1.

National Society of Allotment and Leisure Gardeners Ltd, 22 High Street, Flitwick, Beds.

Northern Horticultural Society, Harlow Car Gardens, Harrogate, North Yorkshire.

National Trust, 42 Queen Anne's Gate, London SW1.

National Vegetable Society, 29 Revidge Road, Blackburn, Lancs.

Saintpaulia and Houseplant Society, 82 Rossmore Court, Park Road, London NW1.

Soil Association Ltd, Walnut Tree Manor, Haughley, Stowmarket, Suffolk. *(Organic gardening)*

Specialist Nurseries

Beth Chatto, Unusual Plants, Elmstead Market, Colchester, Essex. *(Rare and unusual hardy plants and bulbs)*

Washfield Nursery, Hawkhurst, Kent. *(Rare and unusual hardy plants and bulbs)*

Edrom Nurseries, Coldingham, Eyemouth, Berwickshire. *(Alpines and primulas)*

J. & E. Parker-Jervis, Martens Hall Farm, Longworth, Abingdon, Oxon. *(Hardy plants and bulbs, especially snowdrops and colchicums)*
P.J. & J.W. Christian, Pentre Cottages, Minera, Wrexham, Clwyd. *(Alpines and bulbs; hardy orchids)*
Reginald Kaye Ltd, Waithman Nurseries, Silverdale, Lancs. *(Hardy plants, especially ferns)*
Scotts of Merriott, Somerset. *(Rare varieties of fruit tree and bush)*
Chiltern Seeds, Bortree Stile, Ulverston, Cumbria. *(Unusual seeds)*
Great Dixter Nurseries, Northiam, Rye, East Sussex. *(Hardy plants; large list of clematis)*
Fisks Clematis Nursery, Westleton, Saxmundham, Suffolk.
Hollington Nurseries Ltd, Woolton Hill, Newbury, Berks. *(Herbs)*
Peter Beales, London Road, Attleborough, Norfolk. *(Old fashioned roses)*
David Austin, Albrighton, Wolverhampton. *(Old fashioned roses and peonies)*
John Chambers, 15 Westleigh Road, Barton Seagrave, Kettering, Northants. *(Wild flower seeds)*
Helen Ballard, Old Country, Mathon, Malvern, Worcestershire. *(Hellebores and snowdrops)*
Richard Cawthorne, Lower Dalton's Nursery, Swanley Village, Swanley, Kent. *(Violas and violettas)*
Ramparts Nursery, Bakers Lane, Colchester, Essex. *(Grey- and silver-leaved plants)*
W. Robinson & Sons Ltd, Sunnybank, Forton, Preston, Lancs. *(Mammoth show vegetable seeds)*

Acknowledgments

The publishers are grateful for permission to quote from the following books and articles:

Anderson, E.B., *Dwarf Bulbs for the Rock Garden*, Nelson (1959).

Baker, Margaret, *The Gardener's Folklore*, David & Charles (1977).

Bates, H.E., *A Love of Flowers*, Michael Joseph (1971).

Carroll, Lewis, *Alice's Adventures in Wonderland* (1865).

Chatto, Beth, *The Dry Garden*, J.M. Dent (1978).

Coats, Peter, *Great Gardens of the Western World*, Weidenfeld & Nicolson (1963).

Cobbett, William, *Cottage Economy* (1823).

Chinery, Michael, *The Natural History of the Garden*, Collins (1977).

Davidson, William, *The Houseplant Survival Manual*, Hamlyn (1982).

Ellacombe, Canon, *In a Gloucestershire Garden*, E. Arnold (1895).

Finnis, Valerie, *A Gardener's Dozen*, BBC (1980).

Fish, Margery, *We Made a Garden*, Faber (1956).

Lees-Milne, Alvilde and Verey, Rosemary, *The Englishman's Garden*, Allen Lane (1982).

Hall, Sir A. Daniel, *The Apple*, Martin Hopkinson (1933).

Hennig, Frank, *Cheerio Frank, Cheerio Everybody*, Angus & Robertson (1976).

Hessayon, Dr D.G., *The Lawn Expert*, pbi (1982).

Hibberd, Shirley, *The Amateur's Greenhouse and Conservatory*, Groombridge & Sons (1880).

Huxley, Anthony, *House Plants, Cacti and Succulents*, Hamlyn (1972).

Jekyll, Gertrude, *Gardens for Small Country Houses*, Country Life (1912).

Larkcom, Joy, *Vegetables from Small Gardens*, Faber (1976).

Lloyd, Christopher, *The Well Tempered Garden*, Collins (1970).

Loads, Fred, *Gardening Tips of a Lifetime*, Hamlyn (1980).

Pemberton, The Rev. Joseph H., *Roses: Their History, Development and Cultivation*, Longmans (1920).

Potter, Beatrix, *The Tale of Peter Rabbit*, and *The Tale of Jemima Puddleduck* Frederick Warne (1902, 1908).

Sackville-West, Vita, article in the *Journal of the Royal Horticultural Society* (November 1953) and *The Garden*, Heinemann (1946).

Scott-James, Anne, *Down to Earth*, Michael Joseph (1971) and *The Pleasure Garden*, John Murray (1977).

Sutton & Sons, Reading, *The Culture of Vegetables & Flowers*, Simpkin, Marshall, Hamilton, Kent & Co. (1895).

Thrower, Percy, *My Lifetime of Gardening*, Hamlyn (1977).

Titchmarsh, Alan, *Avant-Gardening: A Guide to One-Upmanship in the Garden*, Souvenir Press (1984).

Verey, Rosemary, *The Scented Garden*, Michael Joseph (1981).